Spiritual Logic

or Hints and Helps to Personal Devotions
by Thomas Harrison
with chapters by C. Matthew McMahon

I0079497

Copyright Information

Spiritual Logic or Hints and Helps to Personal Devotions, by Thomas Harrison with chapters by C. Matthew McMahon
Edited by Therese B. McMahon and Susan Ruth

Table of Contents

Spiritual Logic?
by C. Matthew McMahon Ph.D., Th.D.

It may be that Harrison uses this title "Spiritual Logic" to aid the reader in understanding that there is a *logical order* to the way one prays and thinks about their time of personal devotions. To be *logical* is capable of reasoning, or of using reason in an orderly cogent fashion, *i.e.* to be a logical thinker. God is a God of logic, and so, why would someone *not* use logic to "*order* their prayers?"

Prayer is the word of God formed into an argument and retorted back to God again. Most Christians have a hard time with this because that would mean not only would they logically use certain arguments with God in their prayers, but they would have to know their bibles in order to pray. Is this not, at least, one of the reasons that the wicked are abominable in their prayers – they do not know what God requires of them and cannot pray according to the word, which is "in the Holy Spirit" as Jude instructs; *i.e. pray in the Holy Spirit*?

Harrison is going to take you down a *logical* road of gaining some *hints and helps* to your personal devotional life. He will aid you in overcoming an inept prayer life and help you to cultivate your conversations with God in a deeper fashion. He deals with several preliminary aspects that serve as hindrances to good devotions, such as: unacquaintedness with the Lord, a sense of inadequacy, to be unacquainted savingly with God, what it means to be jealous for Christ, to love Christ, and to love the Father in the power of the Spirit. He covers the fear of unbelief, the fear of hypocrisy, the fear of being acted only by a slavish spirit of fear, a sense of fearful backslidings, and a sense of one's strong corruptions that hinder devotions. He speaks extensively of many negative thoughts that crowd the Christian when they try to have faithful devotions, such as desertion felt or feared by God (will God even hear me?), sudden uneasiness that one experiences from cloudy providences, how to deal with the dread of spiritual judgements, hardness of heart, and unprofitableness under the means of grace. Especially considered is the fear that one's prayer is not heard. How many Christians have considered that!

Harrison's work is unique, as he testifies in his *intro*, that he not only gives various remedies for *hindrances*, but also *helps* to devotion in the actual way the Christian ought to logically speak to God by using his phrase (spiritual *logic*) in setting their prayers on God's prescriptions. Then, he concludes his work in looking forward in personal devotion, to become better at it. Christians *grow*.

This is an excellent work in showing, step by step, how the Christian can pray effectively using this *spiritual logic*, which is indeed, hints and helps to personal devotions, during their quiet time with the Lord.

In Christ's grace,
C. Matthew McMahon, Ph.D., Th.D.
From my study, January, 2023.

Meet Thomas Harrison

Edited by C. Matthew McMahon Ph.D., Th.D.

Thomas Harrison D.D. (1618–1682) was a nonconformist divine, born at Kingston-upon-Hull, Yorkshire, and was taken by his parents while a youth to New England, and there trained up to the ministry. He became chaplain to the governor of Virginia, an enemy of the puritans. The governor, with the involvement of Harrison, expelled from Virginia certain ministers who held extreme views, and their expulsion was followed by a disastrous rising among the Indians. This was held by many, Harrison included, to be a judgment of Providence against the persecutors of the expelled preachers. Harrison's change of views occasioned his dismissal, upon which he came to London, and, obtaining some fame as a preacher, was chosen about 1650 to succeed Dr. Thomas Goodwin in his "gathered church" at St. Dunstan's-in-the-East. Here he remained for a few years, after which he removed to Brombrough Hall, Wirrall, Cheshire.

In 1657 he accompanied Henry Cromwell, when he went to Ireland as lord-lieutenant. He lived in Cromwell's family, and preached at Christ Church, Dublin. At the *Restoration* he left Ireland, and settled in Chester, preaching to large congregations in the cathedral, until he was silenced by *the Act of Uniformity*.

From a list of graduates at Cambridge from October 10, 1660 to October 10, 1661, it appears that Harrison earned his *doctorate* there; but according to Edmund Calamy[1] he received it at Dublin. After the passing of the Act of Uniformity he returned to Dublin and founded a flourishing dissenting church of congregational views.

Harrison's eloquence and fluency both in prayer and preaching brought him great notoriety, and Calamy states that "he was a complete gentleman, much courted for his conversation." When he died there was a general mourning in Dublin. He left behind him a valuable library, containing many manuscripts, among them a "System of Divinity" in a large folio written by himself.

Harrison published:

1. Topica Sacra: *Spiritual Logick*: some brief Hints and Helps to Faith, Meditation, and Prayer, Comfort and Holiness. Communicated at Christ Church, Dublin, in Ireland, London, 1658, 12mo. This was dedicated to Henry Cromwell. It became extremely popular during the end of the seventeenth century, especially among the poorer classes in Scotland. A second part was added in 1712 by John Hunter, minister of Ayr. This was frequently reprinted. A revised and corrected edition of the first part, under the title of 'Spiritual Pleadings and Expostulations with God in Prayer,' was published by the Rev. Peter Hall in 1838 in 16mo.

---

[1] *Account*, p. 607

2. "Old Jacob's Account Cast up, etc.," a Funeral Sermon for Lady Susannah Reynolds, preached at Lawrence Jewry, February 13, 1654.

3. "Threni Hibernici, or Ireland sympathising with England and Scotland in a sad Lamentation for the Loss of their Josiah;" a Sermon preached at Christ Church, Dublin, on the Death of Oliver Cromwell, London, 1659, 4to; dedicated to 'the most illustrious Richard, Lord Protector, *etc.*

4. Harrison prefixed 'An Epistle to the Reader' to 'Lemmata Meditationum, *etc.* By Philo-Jesus Philo-Carolus,' Dublin, 1672, 8vo.

For further study: Palmer's *Nonconformist's Memorial*, 1802, i. 330, iii. 174; Wilson's *Hist. of Dissenting Churches*, i. 221–3; *Hist. of the Writers of Ireland*, written in Latin by Sir James Ware, ... translated by Walter Harris, Dublin, 1639, p. 343; *Notes and Queries*, 2nd ser. i. 94, 181.

Preface

To His Excellency, The Lord Henry Cromwell, The Lord Deputy of Ireland

May it please your Excellency,

The reason I allowed this *discourse* to go abroad and not some others is partly to beg pardon for that disobedience, partly to evidence, that it was no defect in my will but rather in my notes and manner of writing that hindered me from paying that observance which now I yield. But especially because the Spirit of God by these and similar injections and intimations, helping me to plead and press them, to hold them up before the Lord, and to spread them before him as Hezekiah did the letter, has many times sustained and cheered my own heart. For when God speaks, where are the lips that will not quiver at his voice?

This gives me some small glimmer of hope that the same powerful Spirit may be pleased also to manage and improve the same medium to the relief and advantage of others. And I can say it is usefulness and service that I have aimed at in this enterprise.

Among all the *helps to devotion* that I have seen, I cannot remember anything at all of this kind to this undertaking which tends to help the gift and not stint the Spirit of prayer.

Whatever strangers, either in place or affection may imagine, I know your Excellency to be a pleader, and (I hope) a prevailer with God daily.

I therefore offer this poor *essay* to you, not so much by way of assistance but as acknowledgement that under God you have been and are the instrumental cause of my enjoying a fulness of opportunities, of doing some service in my generation; the value of which I desire daily to renew on my heart above all the things that this world can afford or brittle mortality enjoy.

As it has been your Lordship's mercy, that here you have had help from on high to know and love the Lord, his name and image wherever you discern it, and to walk acceptably with your God and usefully to his people. So it is now become your obligation and only interest, still to be found in the same ways of righteousness in which you may persevere to the end and that your path may be as the shining light which shines out more and more to the perfect day! That you, your most precious consort and hopeful children, may prove an inestimable blessing in this world and eternally blessed in that to come, is, and shall be the daily prayer of,

Your Excellencies' worthless but most willing servant.
THOMAS HARRISON

Chapter 1: Introduction

Job 23:3-4, "O That I knew where I might find him, that I might come even to his seat! I would order my cause before him and fill my mouth with arguments."

Holy Job, poor now even to a proverb, and miserable to a prodigy, perceiving his friend's discourses fuller of reproaches then consolations, neglects to answer them and resolves to pursue God, the only support and refuge of the miserable. And in this way, he entertains himself in the second verse, "even today after all that has been said, the bitterness of my complaint is rather increased than allayed; wherefore no wonder my mouth is always open to breathe out complaints. And yet the more I complain, the more I suffer from you or rather from God himself, whose hand I acknowledge in all these strokes. Let me complain as long as I will. My tongue is not so eloquent in complaining as his hand is heavy that strikes me; my stroke is heavier than my groaning."

And yet for all this, verse 3, after a nearer access and approach to him that *smites* him, he quits his *seeming* friends to make after his *seeming* enemy and is willing to make this enemy his Judge and to refer everything to him.

And then in verse 4, he thinks with himself how he would manage his matters, how he would not lose his cause for lack of pleading, if he could only get a day of hearing; "I would order my cause before him and fill my mouth with arguments."

Some think he wishes for a guide, a *friend* to help him to such an opportunity. He would gladly find an angel to conduct him to the throne of God or rather the Angel of the Covenant to allow him that access which the Apostle speaks of, as the known privilege of all believers who through him have *an access by one Spirit unto the Father*, (Eph. 2:18).

But not to darken the words instead of explaining them, by giving the various readings and opinions of interpreters, I will draw out some observations and hasten to that which I desire to insist on.

Observation 1. The sorest strokes cannot drive away good souls from God, but will rather draw them nearer to him. "My stroke is heavier than my groaning; yet O that I knew where I might find him!" God himself, even for his own sake, is the great Object of a saint's seeking. *O that I knew where I might find him...* and not this or that to be gotten by him.

Precious souls that have a large interest in God are sometimes at a loss, as to his *sweet* and *sensible* presence. The great God has his unknown retreats, where even his best friends cannot follow him. So Job 23:8-9, "Behold, I go forward, but he is not there; and backward, but I cannot perceive him; on the left hand, where he doth work, but I cannot behold him; he hides himself on the right hand that I cannot see him." So holy David says in Psalm 63:1, "O God, thou art my God, early will I seek thee." You see his interest is clear; he can say, "Thou art my God," and yet he had but little enjoyment of him. His soul *thirsts, longs, follows hard after him* (verse 8). Such another sigh you have in Psalm 101:2, "O when will you come to me? Do not conclude you have no interest because you have little enjoyment, no union because you lack vision." A gracious heart seldom or never thinks itself near enough to God, its sun and shield and center. "O that I knew where I might find him, that I might come even to his seat!"

Even God's judgment seat where he sits to hear and determine causes is not terrible or unapproachable to a believer who knows it to be a throne of mercy, as Job here did. For he says in verse 6, *how would he respond to me if he had me there? Would he overwhelm me with his greatness? Will he plead against me with his absolute power? No, but he would put strength in me.* Happy are all that can say so, for we must all appear there (2 Cor. 5:10-11), and it will be terrible to all those that do not often resort there beforehand.

A poor afflicted creature often thinks he has a great deal to say to God if he could but get a hearing. He thinks how he would order and argue on the matter. What a story he would tell if he could but get his ear, gain access and audience from him. I tell you that it is good to have our hearts and mouths filled with arguments when we come to plead and explain and reason out our great concerns with God.

Chapter 2:
Breaking the Spirit of Slumber

This is the point I want to focus on, to expel that spirit of slumber which has so weakened the spirit of prayer that those who trade to heaven with it, where God has all good things lying ready by him, waiting only for prayer to come and fetch them away, are by comparison little enriched by it.

When Christ himself would give us a perfect pattern of prayer, both for matter and manner, he winds and wraps up all this with a conclusion in Matthew 6:13 consisting of certain reasons to persuade God to hear our prayers, or at least to persuade and assure ourselves that he does and will hear them. The reasons bear influence into all and every one of the petitions. *Thine is the kingdom*, and therefore we expect that as a good King you should receive and answer our petitions. It is your concern as a King to have your honor advanced, therefore hallow your one name, glorify it in the church, let your kingdom come to it, advance your will in it, sustain us as your subjects, pardon our sins, keep and defend us from evils. So *Thine is the power*, which kings oftentimes lack. But you are able to exalt your own name, to extend your kingdom over all, to fit us to do your will, to minister to our necessities, to pardon our sins, to preserve us from *all* evils.

And *thine is the glory*; the hallowing of your name is the chief part of your glory. Your kingdom is the prime place of your glory; in this you are glorified when we obey your will, when you provide for your people, forgive their sins, preserve and deliver them from their enemies. Therefore, do all these things for us, for we trust and hope that you will do all these things for us. In this way our blessed Savior directs us, and in this way the blessed saints have practiced in all ages.

When the people of Israel made the golden calf and committed idolatry with it, and God was about to destroy them for it, see how Moses in his prayer for them lays hold on the avenging hand of God, and he even stays it by reasoning and arguing – from the dishonor that would redound to God if he should destroy them and from the covenant that he had made with their fathers in Exodus 32:11-13, "And Moses besought the Lord his God, and said, Lord, why doth thy wrath wax hot against thy people which thou hast brought forth out of the Land of Egypt with great power and with a mighty hand? The Egyptians will slander thy gracious intentions, and say it was for mischief with a purpose to slay and consume them. Remember Abraham, Isaac and Israel thy servants, to whom thou swore by thine own self that thou would deal otherwise with their posterity." And see how he prevails, "The Lord repented of the evil which he thought to do unto his people," (verse 14). So when he would have destroyed them for murmuring, Moses interposed again for a pardon, and fills his mouth with arguments. "The Egyptians will hear it, and they will tell stories of you to the inhabitants of this land, and they will slander your power, and say, because you were not able to carry them any further, you rid thy hands of them in the wilderness. Now therefore I beseech you, show what you can do, put forth the greatness of your power in pardoning, as you have spoken of yourself, and as you have practiced heretofore in forgiving this people from Egypt even until now." And see how he carries it again in verse 20, "The Lord said, I have pardoned according to thy word."

Likewise Abraham before him in Genesis 18:23-25, "Will you also destroy the righteous with the wicked? Be that far from thee to do after this manner, to slay the righteous with the wicked, and that the righteous should be as the wicked, be that far from thee. Shall not the judge of all the earth do right?" And you know how he reduced and narrowed the number until he thought he had gotten within the number of Lot's family, expecting that should at least allow for the number of righteous persons he named. But he was outside the number he pleaded for; otherwise he would not have failed in what he pleaded for. He gained ground at every advance, and God yielded until Abraham thought he had enough, and so pressed him no further.

And again Joshua, when the people were smitten at Ai, (Joshua 7:7-9), "Alas, O Lord God, wherefore have you brought us at all over Jordan? Or was it our ambition and covetousness that brought us over? Would to God we had been content and dwelt on the other side Jordan. O Lord God, what shall I say when Israel turns their backs before their enemies! And now they will all hear of it, and surround us, and cut off our name from the earth. But what will you do to your great Name?" As if he were to say, that will hardly swim if ours sink, they are so twisted together; and though ours is vile, yours is precious. Think what you are about to do to your great Name.

Hezekiah pleads with the Lord in his sickness (Isa. 38:2-3), "Remember now O Lord, I beseech thee, how I have walked before thee in truth: I have had an honest heart towards you and you know it; and must I now be cut off untimely? When all things are so unsettled, now or never is the time for you to give testimony to my sincerity." And God answered by adding 15 years to his life (verse 4). In this way he argues in his distress because of Sennacherib (2 Kings 19:15), "They have indeed made work with the gods of the nations, and cast them into the fire, because they were no gods. But now that they come to meddle with thee and thy people, let them find it too hot for them, and let all the kingdoms of the earth know that thou art the Lord God, even thou only."

In this way Asa in 2 Chron. 14:11, "O Lord our God, we rest on thee, thou art our God, let not man prevail against thee."

In this way Jehoshaphat in 2 Chron. 20, Daniel (Dan. 9), Amos (Amos 7: 2-6), and the Apostles (Acts 4:24-31).

Not that God *needs* us to inform him concerning our necessities, which he knows better than we, but because hereby we give some proof that we are not altogether strangers. Rather, we know something of ourselves, and our own cases, and of him and his dealings towards us. But I will give no other grounds for the point than those of Job's resolution for this practice; and they are these.

Upon earnest arguing God will undoubtedly answer some way or another. This is implied in verse 5, "I would know the words that he would answer me and understand what he would say unto me." In other words, I may be sure of an answer when I fill my mouth with arguments; he will not sit still and say nothing. He will not sit like an image, like a dumb idol, as the abominations of the heathens and their dunghill gods (as they are called in Deut. 29:17) must of necessity do. They can do nothing more, even though men fill their mouths with arguments and empty their veins of their blood before them (1 Kings 18:28).

As Job argues, he will undoubtedly answer if I sufficiently plead, and I might guess at his designs by his answers (which are now too wonderful for me). I might understand why he contends with me and what he means and intends towards his poor creature.

Arguments, then, in prayer are not likely to go unanswered, and praying souls find it so.

Sometimes he answers gloriously from his secret place of thunder, though not in thunder but in lightning, in some glorious irradiation, in some precious promise born in upon the heart that melts it with a strong hand and there engraved in indelible characters by an irresistible power, of which gracious souls have had abundant experience.

Sometimes he answers in some secret support only, as Hannah after arguing and pouring forth her sorrowful soul into his bosom, leaving her petition in his hand or laying it down at his feet. She had no other fiat than what was written on her heart by an invisible finger, yet she went her way well paid, and her countenance was no more sad (1 Sam. 1:18).

And surely one or the other of these made David end so many Psalms with praises and rejoicings which he had begun with tears and mourning. An obvious observation and clear evidence that even while he was on his knees before the Lord, the wind came about and blew upon him out of a warm corner and made all his spices flow.

Sometimes God answers in some providential dispensations, which both gratify us for the present and instruct us for the future. For many, very many providences are prophetical and show us things to come. But the language of prophecies is for the most part obscure, and we seldom understand it until God interprets it in the accomplishment. We have such an example in Acts 7:25. Moses was defending the Israelite and avenging him that was oppressed when he killed the Egyptian. That act of vindication held the seed of a future where God would deliver the oppressed children of Israel from the hand of pharaoh through his servant Moses. But his Jewish brethren did not understand that, no more than we understand the full extent and import of a dispensation which echoes back to prayer. Plead then and fill your mouths with arguments; for whenever you do so, it may just be that God will answer.

Secondly, there is no fear that he will interpret your pleading arguments as presumptions and in so doing beat you about the face or kick you out of his presence. There is no fear that he will smother you under the weight of his greatness, or dazzle you with his beams, or burn you with his flames, or drive you from the judgment seat. No, he never beats his people lower than their knees, and in this way allows them, yes even helps them, to rise again. He will lay his hand upon your head and under your feet to do you good. He will stroke rather than strike a pleading soul; he will strengthen you and put strength into you. This is Job's consideration in the sixth verse, "Will he plead against me with his great and absolute power, by which he may do what he pleases with his poor creatures? Will he serve me so? No, but he would put strength in me."

Thirdly, there the righteous may plead and dispute with him, even at the *Bar* of Equity and Justice, and the Judge cannot but pronounce and pass sentence in their favor. This encouragement is found in verse 7, "there the righteous may plead with him, and so shall I be delivered forever from my Judge," never more to dread him as a Judge but to love him and live with him as a Father.

There righteous Jeremiah pleads with him (Jer. 12:1), "Righteous art thou O Lord when I plead with you," (there's no question of that), yet let me talk with you of your judgments.

There he invites his people to come and plead freely as in Isaiah 43:26, "Put me in remembrance, let us plead together, declare you that you may be justified." If you have anything to say for yourself, say on. For even idolaters shall have permission to plead for themselves, as well as for their dumb idols too, if they have anything to say for them (Isa. 41:21). Produce your cause, says the Lord. Bring forth your strong reasons, says the King of Jacob. Do idolaters have this liberty, and not the worshippers of the true God that worship in spirit and truth? Shall the wicked have this privilege and not the righteous? Yes doubtless, this is that privilege of the saints found in Heb. 10:19, "having therefore boldness to enter into the holiest by the blood of Jesus," (a right and freedom to enter in our persons hereafter, and now by our prayers, given us by the death and resurrection of Christ), "let us draw near with a true heart, in full assurance of faith."

Chapter 3: Praying to God

[Objection 1] But some may ask, where are those righteous ones? And who are *they*? For it is not so with me. God be merciful to me a grievous sinner; I dare not be so bold with him.

I answer, everyone that has a share in, yea a sincere desire after the righteousness of Christ, is righteous before him and may in that righteousness plead and prevail, and as a prince have power with God. For this is the righteousness of God's own contrivance and appointment: the righteousness which is of God by faith, (Phil. 3:8-9). This is a righteousness spun and woven out of his own bowels, and the obedience of his dear Son, evangelical being far better than angelical righteousness. To be certain, you cannot miss a blessing while clothed in the garments of him who is not ashamed to be called your elder brother. He came to change places with you and to take all upon himself so that you might escape. The Father cannot but be well pleased with the smell of his Son's raiment. He sits upon a seat of judgment and must do you right, and justice itself (which will not be twice paid) is as much for you and is as much your friend as is mercy. As Rom. 3:26 states, "He is just, and a justifier of him that believes on Jesus." So that if you are not utterly shut up in unbelief, if there is but the least spark of true faith alive in your heart, you yourself, my friend, may plead and prosper.

[Objection 2] But I have nothing to say for myself. My heart is dried up like a potshard and withered like grass.

I have sinned away all arguments and must never open my mouth any more before him.

True, you cannot *boast*. But you may certainly *plead*.

And have you nothing to offer? Not the groanings of your soul? *O that I knew where I might find him!* Where the heart is as full as Job's was, the mouth will not be empty. A full heart will fill the mouth some way or other. If the heart is full of affection, the mouth will be full of *arguments*. Psalm 37:30 says, "the mouth of the righteous speaks wisdom, and his tongue talks of judgment." And why so? Verse 31 explains, "the Law of his God is in his heart." This is what sets his tongue going the right way. The language of sighs and groans is powerful rhetoric, so let the sighing of the prisoners come before you (Psa. 79:11) according to the greatness of your power preserve those who are appointed to die. And for the oppression of the poor and the sighing of the needy, now will I arise, says the Lord (Psa. 12:5). Likewise the Spirit also helps our infirmities; for we do not know what we should pray for. And yet the Spirit itself makes intercession for us with groanings which cannot be uttered (Rom. 8:26). He is both an *Interpreter* (as his title signifies, as well as *Comforter*) to make known the mind of God to us and ours to him. Further, it is he who fills the mouths of the saints not only with windy words but also weighty arguments.

Have you nothing to complain of to your Judge? No sin, no devil, no diabolical temptations, no super diabolical corruption, no spiritual plunderers, no Egyptian taskmasters, no cruel bondage that makes life bitter to you?

No enemy coming in as a flood to oppress and do you wrong? No iron yoke that breaks your shoulders? No violence and spoil to cry out and complain of? Surely you have not studied your own case, have not ordered your cause rightly, if this fountain fails you.

But will this be admitted? Those who are poor may say that all complaints are troublesome; men cannot endure them. But God can, and he will. "Out of the abundance of my complaint and grief have I spoken," says Hannah (1 Sam. 1:16).

The word rendered "arguments," in terms of our English translation of the word (and this is warranted by the best critics) signifies all proceedings, all arguments, and reasons used in a cause, by either party, and contains all that can be alleged or urged by a poor creature any way in his own defense or for his advantage.

There are some arguments archived in the rolls and records of heaven which were never yet unveiled; they lie in the Ark of the Covenant, hid with Christ in God (under double lock and key) where neither moth nor rust can come to corrupt nor thief break through to steal. Yea, they lie (many of them) in the very heart and bosom and being of God himself. I hope we shall meet with some of them presently, and that your soul may meet with God in making use of them.

[Objection 3] But what arguments will work upon God? That King Eternal is not swayed but by eternal considerations. He knows no motives but his own and the merits and mediation of his Son and Spirit.

This is true, and it is good for you and me that it is so. Otherwise the accidents and exacerbations of time itself would have well before now ushered us into eternity!

Has he not given you those two great friends of his for your advocates? His Son at his own right hand in heaven moving and negotiating, and always appearing for you, and the other seated in your heart? To be sure, the Father's own heart is full of love, brimming full and running over upon you, and by this continually pleads for you, causing all your arrows to fly upwards; not one is shot in vain.

Good arguments in prayer know the necessity of prayer as well as the great equity we have for obtaining the things prayed for. By doing so, these arguments very much confirm our faith and fire our affections, and enable a man to break through many discouragements which Satan or his own heart may throw in to hinder prayer. Though there is no need for arguments to work upon God, there is certainly a need for them to work upon us. They do not work to move his love but rather to remove our unbelief. They do not prevail upon him to give so much as to prepare our own hearts to receive mercy.

The only use I shall make of this point is to press all of us to make use of it, to put it in practice daily. It will please your Heavenly Father very well, for he loves to hear his children reason it out with him. Not only that, he may delay granting our requests sometimes because he loves to hear often from us, to hear our voices and see our faces. He loves to hear what they can say for themselves. Recall this is how Christ dealt with the woman of Canaan. He first seemed not to hear her, then he denied her suit. And finally gave a very sharp and cutting reason for his denial, because she was a "dog," (a Samaritan), and not one of the Israelites who were his children. But when Christ hears her wise answer to his objection: "This is true, Lord, but the dogs eat of the crumbs that fall from their master's table," (a strong piece of logic) she received a high commendation of her faith, and a grant that would be sure to please her. "O woman great is thy faith, be it unto thee even as you will," (Matt. 15:21-22). She uses his own weapon upon him, and he yields and gives her what is even potentially dangerous instead, which is to say, her own will.

Chapter 4: Being Acquainted with God

My purpose here is to speak to some principal cases of greatest concern and most frequent occurrence in our lives. Or in the apostle's phrase, to stir up the fire which lies raked up and buried under the ashes of laziness. And to also jog the spirit of prayer which lies dormant in many bosoms and does them little service. I would but set that plow moving again which too many cast in the hedge as almost useless. And yet, this same plow of prayer, if well managed, would fill your garners with all manner of store. For whoever puts his hand to it, without looking back, shall be fit for the Kingdom of God.

First then, is an *unacquaintedness with God.* Is this your complaint, that you hear so little from him? That neither the thunder of his power, nor the charms of his love are sufficiently understood by you? We are known by him, but can we say of him that we know him? (Gal. 4:9). Some make this to be the case with Job, "O that I knew God, then I should find him." He that knows God has found him; and he shall never find him who never knows him. His friend that last advised him, (Job 22:21), said, "Acquaint now thyself with him, and be peace," to which Job answers, "O that I knew him, O that I knew where I might find him to be better acquainted with him." Is this your case? Then go order your cause before him and fill your mouth with arguments.

Ask him (with a humble and holy boldness) if he is not willing to be known? Does he make darkness his pavilion round about him? And if so, then why has he made intelligent beings capable of knowing him; and eternally miserable if they know him not?

Why has he written and declared such admirable comments and characteristics and attributes of himself regarding the invisible things of God, his eternal power and Godhead?

Why has he sparkled forth such glorious discoveries in the sacred Scriptures in the face of Jesus Christ! In the births and breathings, the hints and whispers of his Spirit, the ways and workings of his providence, the experience of all his saints, and yea in your own heart, mind, and soul, dark and dolesome though it may be.

Why has he so often laid his commands upon poor sinners to seek him, if he means not to be found? Show him his own hand for it, "Thus saith the Lord to the house of Israel, seek ye me and ye shall live," (Amos 5:4). "Seek the Lord, and ye shall live," (verse 6), and yet again, in verse 8, "Seek him that makes the seven stars and Orion and turns the shadow of death into the morning." What does all this earnestness mean if he does not mean to be found? Is not this the very reason he gives life and breath to all things, that they should seek the Lord, for "if haply they might find him, though he be not far from every one of us," (Acts 17:27).

Ask him if he has not been found of many a soul that sought him not? Did not he prevent them himself? Is there a soul with him now in heaven whose name is not sought out? (Isa. 62:12). And will he now hide himself from one that seeks him?

Ask him how is it that you now have a heart to seek him? Is it not because he has found you and means to be found of you? (Jer. 29:12-14). He knows that your whole heart is, or would be, engaged in this work.

Why does he allow so long a time to seek him in? All the time of this life as some think, at least until in his wrath one's heart is judicially hardened. And yet this is not your case because through infinite mercy you are not bound among the damned.

Tell him, (if it is indeed so), that you would be acquainted with him not merely to gratify a natural itch after knowledge and not only so that you might talk of him, but rather that you could walk with him, and love him, and fear him, and obey him in all things. Even in natural things, the hand contributes more to knowledge then the brain, for those things we learn to do, we learn by doing them. So it is with spiritual things, as Christ said in John 7:17, "If any man will do his will, he shall know of the doctrine."

Lastly, tell him it is not in a fit of new-found excitement that you are ambitious of his acquaintance, but rather he knows you have been of this mind for many a day, you have pursued knowing him and now you expect that good word of his should be made good unto your soul. As Hosea 6:3 says, "Then shall we know if we follow on to know the Lord; his going forth is prepared as the morning; and he shall come unto us as the rain, as the later and former rain unto the earth." Press these things upon him and his love and truth will let him hide no longer.

Does the sense of your more than ordinary unworthiness oppress you? Does the horrid realization of your sins weigh heavy as a mountain of lead upon your soul and stifle all the moving and mountings of your spirit upward? Does this nip all the buddings and blooming of faith and hope, and force you often to sigh in secret, "It is impossible for me to be saved, I shall certainly at last prove myself to be a reprobate!" Is this your case? Go plead your case before him, and still your soul with arguments to him. In all humility ask him if he did not (before the foundations of the world were laid) choose voluntarily, absolutely and immutably what company he would have with him to all eternity. And then if you sometimes think he would never have chosen you, study that point a little and get it removed.

He was under no necessity to choose anyone of us. He might have chosen whether ever there should have been such a body of Christ at all. God the Father begets the Son necessarily, not arbitrarily; that is, from his nature, not from his good pleasure. But he chooses him to be the head and root and representative of the Church arbitrarily, not necessarily; this is from his good pleasure, not from his nature. How free is he then in all his other elections?

He chose in deed in Christ, but not for Christ. As in the natural birth, so here the head comes forth first, and then the members. Christ is the cause of the salvation of the elect, but not of election to salvation, for that is God's doing. And there can be no cause of God; God cannot be an effect. As Christ himself acknowledged in John 17:6, "Thine they were, and thou gave them to me."

God did not choose immediately to salvation, for that was too great a stride at once. But to *sanctification of the Spirit unto obedience* (2 Thess. 2:13, 1 Pet. 1:2), not because he foresaw that some would be holy, but that they might be so (Eph. 1:4). The great plot was how to conform sinful creatures to the image of his Son, (Rom. 8:29). Go then and put him to it; ask him if he will own this doctrine, and seal it upon your heart.

Secondly, tell him that by condemning he glorifies only one or two of his attributes – justice and sovereignty. But in saving he will magnify them all.

Thirdly, remind him how often he has already sacrificed to his justice by punishing offenders of his grace. Hell is full of those sacrifices, and yet the sufferings of his Son do more to display the glory of his holiness than them all, than all the everlasting torments of the damned.

Fourthly, ask him if heaven will not afford plenty of precedents for similar mercies you now need and beg of him.

Fifthly, ask him if he means to let slip such an opportunity to set forth the greatness and transcendency of his grace and mercy in all its pomp and power. And then fill your heart and mouth with the same argument as found in Psalm 25:11, "For thy name's sake, O Lord, pardon mine iniquity, for it is great." This is indeed a good argument, for it seems David thought so, and so did Moses in Exodus 32:31, "This people has sinned a great sin!" But here's work now for the greatness of God's power in pardoning. As Num. 14:17 states, "and now I beseech thee let the power of my Lord be great according as thou hast spoken."

To honor his Son in reconciling us to himself, God permits the greatest sins and enmities to be in the hearts and lives of those he intends to save. And you may well know that God will not be lacking in terms of glorifying his own grace and his Son's merits, and the pardoning of such great and grievous sins will serve abundantly to illustrate and manifest his grace. For the apex of Christ's glory is that he is *able* to save to the *uttermost* those who *come unto God by him*, (Heb. 7:25).

Tell him he shall be more admired and loved for such a miracle of matchless mercy, than for all his curious works of creation or dreadful acts of vengeance.

Tell him it must be no small matter, no easy or ordinary thing that must beget eternal admirations, for the greatest wonders of this world last but just a little while. So those wonders of the next world must last forever. And the pardoning and purifying, the sanctifying and saving of such a sinner will eternally yield oil to such a flame.

Tell him no soul in heaven shall admire or love him more than you (though now you may be the least of his admirers!) for he will love much who is forgiven much.

Lastly, tell him that the wonder shall not be confined to your person, but run through heaven and affect all men and angels, and that (in all likelihood) many shall wonder more for his grace to you than to themselves, who never sinned as much nor in the same manner as your own transgressions. Especially angels that never sinned, how could they know the extent of grace, were it not for such superlative sinners as yourself.

Chapter 5: Secret Fears

The end of philosophy is said to be to admire nothing, but the end and scope of divinity is to make us admire God in everything, and in this thing especially, the eternal salvation of the greatest sinners.

If you have any secret fears that this Lord Jesus whom you have heard and talked so often of takes no notice of you, has no mind to do anything for you, then plead your case, make your arguments before him.

Ask him what made him take so great a journey? What brought him down from heaven to earth? Was it not to seek and to save such lost stray creatures as yourself, who all fall to the Lord of the soul?

Ask him why he invites all weary burdened poor souls to *come unto him*, why he commands them to *cast themselves upon him* and even threatens those who do not with peril and punishment, if he is not willing to bid those that come welcome? After all, the great quarrel between him and sinners is this, "you will not come unto me that you might have life," (John 5:40).

Tell him you believe he would never cast out any one soul that came unto him according to that blessed Word of his. As John 6:37 says, "All that the Father gives me, shall come unto me, and him that comes I will in no wise cast out." Such a text has been a sanctuary to many a troubled soul. Ask him now if he means to begin with you... choosing that you should be the first that ever was refused by him?

Tell him he knows all things; he knows that you do not come to him in pretense. He knows you do not follow him for loaves, for outward advantage and accommodations, because preferment waits upon profession.

Tell him that necessity requires you to come to him, because otherwise you are lost and ruined for all eternity; and yet he knows how valuable your soul is to him, that you look on him as the one thing needful, the more excellent way, and that all your treasures, pleasures, honors, yes, and all that you have are as a drop in the bucket, neither here nor there, in comparison to him.

Lastly, say to him that though it is of necessity, it is also of choice that you come to him. And even if it were possible to be saved any other way, you would still choose him. There was a time when your heart wandered about, a time when you would have gone to any door for relief than his. But since you have had some glances and glimmerings of him, as through a glass or a window or a lattice, since tasting some small drops of his sweetness, he knows your heart is so taken with his glory and grace that you will never go elsewhere. Having been delivered with the love and lovely person of a Savior, even if salvation were only the deliverance from the wrath to come, you could do nothing else. But surely, a full reward shall be given you of the Lord God of Israel, under whose wings you have come to trust.

But it may be that you are well satisfied concerning the freeness and forwardness of Christ to help you. He has suffered enough to convince you such that you have very soft and sweet thoughts of him, and yet terrible ones concerning the Father, for you look upon him as an angry God, an incensed judge and enraged enemy, with his hand always up and ready to strike. But then Christ steps in and thwarts the blow. You believe the Father stands more in the background, for you don't know what to think of him. If this is your case now, and you have misgivings about the Father in your heart, go order your cause before him and fill your mouth with arguments.

First, ask him if that sweet Son of his is not simply as he himself is, the brightness of his glory and the express image of his person (Heb. 1:3).

Of course, Christ as the sinner's friend was affable enough, kind enough, compassionate enough, showed love enough to poor sinners in all his carriage and conversation as well as in his life and in his death. And if you think he was not enough, where and who is he that will come and show more? And yet Christ himself said, "my Father is just such another as I am to a hair's breadth. His heart is as full of love and tenderness as my own. So if you know one, you know both." John 10:30, "I and my Father are one." And John 12:44-45, "Jesus cried out, 'He that believeth on me, believeth not on me but on him that sent me; and he that sees me, sees him that sent me.'" And John 14:9, "Jesus said unto him, 'Have I been so long time with you, and yet you have not known me, Philip? He that has seen me has seen the Father, and how do you then say, show us the Father?'" And, "I came out of his bosom on purpose to declare him," (John 1:18), to be his living Word and light to this dark world.

Was it not God the Father who first summoned that great council held by all the Persons of the Trinity, when neither man nor angel existed? There he sat in consultation with his Wisdom and Love, his Word and Spirit, especially regarding man's salvation. Can that blessed womb miscarry with any of its conceptions? Surely no.

Was it not God who first appointed the Son, establishing him as the foundation to the whole fabric if the universe? One able to bear up the weight of all the work of redemption and mighty to save? And if the angels shouted for joy to see the cornerstone of the earth laid (Job 38:7), shall not the saints with delight see the cornerstone of their salvation laid by the hand of the Father? Then ask him, are you not to have a place in this building?

Was it not God who then took particular cognizance of things and persons, called in Scripture "God's foreknowledge?" (Rom. 8:29, 11:1-2). Was it not enough to overwhelm a poor sinner when he comes to get an inkling of it, that he was then reminded, "did you then think of me? And do you open your eyes upon such a one as me?" (Job 14:3).

Was it not God who then chose whom he would confirm among the angels, calling them the Elect Angels? (1 Tim. 5:21). And though they were never out of favor, yet they are said to be reconciled by running under the wing of Christ, receiving and owning him as their head (Col. 2:10). God would not keep an angel in heaven who was not beholding to his Son for it. So then ask how you may make your own *calling and election sure*.

Was it not God who ratified his choice by a solemn decree, called the *Purpose of God* according to election? (Rom. 9:11), the *Mystery of his Will* according to his good pleasure which he had purposed in himself (Eph. 1:9), the *Eternal Purpose* which he purposed in Christ Jesus our Lord (Eph. 3:11). And yet there is no unrighteousness with God (Rom. 9:14), no cruelty, no dissimulation, no tyranny. And if the Lord has purposed it, who shall disannul it? (Isa. 14:24, 27).

Was it not God who called for the books and caused all the resolves to be entered, (Heb. 10:5), even to the very names written in the Lamb's Book of Life, (Rev. 13:8; 21:27) with the golden letters of love, indelible characters in his blood? Had you ever had any help reading your name written in heaven, this is a matter of more joy than if you could cast out devils and work wonders, (Luke 10:20). Go to the Father and he will help you spell your name there by his Spirit of adoption, who was, and is, a member of this Council and well acquainted with all that passed there.

Was it not God who ordered all things in a way of subordination and subserviency to the sanctification and salvation of the elect? Good works then received his seal (Eph. 2:10). He then drew up the ordinances of heaven, passed a decree for the sea and for the rain, and for the opening of the eyelids of the morning, to cause the dayspring to know its place and the sun his going down (unless forbidden, as in the days of Joshua). He then appointed natural agents to act necessarily; the sun to shine, the fire to burn, the sea to run in its course, with the ability to stop them at his pleasure.

Free moral agents act freely; the will of man is always free in all its acts, to do good or evil at his pleasure (*i.e.* whatever the disposition of his heart is). And yet he need never do evil unless he pleases, so that he is without excuse.

And all other things were ordered as scaffolds to this building. Now who but a mad man would lay his bed on the scaffold and say that's accommodation enough; and so take up with that, no matter the building? Pray that he would ever lead you to things spiritual and eternal, by all externals, and that all things work together for your good, according to this ancient appointment.

Was it not by an agreement between him and his Son, that he should sit as creditor in heaven and that the Son come down to be responsible for justice? There was love enough in his heart to have let the Son sit as creditor in heaven, and to come down himself to die for you. And therefore said Christ, though I should not pray for you, the Father himself loves you (John 16:27). In fact, he loves you so well that he therefore loves me, because I lay down my life for you (John 10:17). What a strange expression of love is this?

Did he not draw up all the Son's articles and instructions, *as:*

1. That he must begin his work in deepest humiliation and abasement.

2. That he must give up his glory to go through with the plan of redemption (John 17:4-5).

3. That his Godhead must be veiled, and he be made like his brethren in their natural necessities, sinless

infirmities, having to live by faith, get everything by prayer; not do his own will but the will of him who sent him and so fulfill all righteousness. Why was he in this way conformed to us ... so that we might be made conformable unto him?

4. That he must in the days of his flesh orally and personally declare his Father's name and love to his brethren; and afterwards commission others to do it to the end of the world. And so long as his league of ambassadors reside in any place not called home, the *Treaty of Peace* holds and continues. And their work is not only to declare Christ, but the Father also. This was the sweetest promise that Christ could cheer up his disciples with. As John 16:25 says, "the time comes when I shall no longer speak unto you in proverbs, but I shall show you plainly of the Father."

5. That he must die a bloody, painful, shameful cursed death to pay the debts of his people and then rise again from the dead, bringing up his blood with him into the Holiest of Holies, and there exercise and execute the office of his everlasting priesthood. If he would have his death which was of infinite value in itself be of infinite virtue and efficacy to others, is not all this performed exactly? And has he not commended his love to us with a witness? (Rom. 5:8).

6. That whatever was given him, he must presently give of the same to his members, to equip them for that glorious fellowship whereunto they are ordained. For what he receives with one hand, he must give with the other. And what David calls receiving, (Psa. 68:18), Paul calls giving, (Eph. 4:12) as if these were one and the same with Christ.

After the Father, (whose motion and project this was), had determined the Son to undertake it, did he not then engage to stand by him and to supply him with all necessaries: a body to suffer in and a spirit to that body without measure, and to bring those to him whom he had given him? He does more than invite; he effectually draws by an omnipotent sweetness. Further, Christ does not fail to entertain the most leprous loathsome sinner whom the Father is pleased to bring to him. And the Father must help to keep them also, whom he has brought in, (John 10:28-29).

Over and above all this, did he not put forth his paternal authority and lay his commands upon his Son, to engage in this great service, (John 10:18)? Can you not believe that Christ loves you enough to lay down his life for you, but can you also believe he loves the Father? There is certainly no doubt of that. Why? "That the world may know how I love the Father as the Father has given me commandment, even so do I," (John 14:31).

Does not the Father engage to reward him plentifully, to give him a royal and an everlasting priesthood, a name above every name, appoint him a kingdom, (Luke 22:29), and above all, assure him of the salvation of those he died for, according to this agreement (Isa. 53:11) without which nothing could ever have satisfied him? So as the assumption of human nature is the highest instance of free mercy, so is the rewarding in its state of exaltation the highest instance of remunerative justice.

All this was needed not to engage Christ to the work so much as to engage us to believe that the Father was willing to make the Son second to him therein. But as they are both equally God, they must necessarily be one in will who are so in nature and being. Nevertheless, the Father is still first in love. As John 3:16 states, "For God so love the world, that he gave his only begotten Son, that whosoever believeth in him should not perish, but have everlasting life." And 1 John 4:9-10, "In this was manifested the love of God towards us, because that God sent his only begotten Son into the world, that we might live through him; herein is love, not that we loved God, but that he loved us, and sent his Son to be the propitiation for our sins." The grace of Christ makes way for our enjoying the love of God; but we had never known the grace of Christ had it not been first for the love of God, who therefore is called our Savior, (1 Tim. 1:1).

And as if all this were not enough, did not the Father commission his Son to give life to lost sinners? (John 6:27). Therefore Christ so often mentions the Father as sending him and furnishing him with miracles, which were his letters of credential wherever he went.

If suffering for our sakes is a sign of love after the manner of men, does not the Father have his share of sufferings as well as the Son? Was it nothing for him to part with his Son? Such a Son, an only Son, the delight of his heart and eyes, and that not among friends but enemies? Is all this nothing? He may seem indeed to have an easy role to sit in heaven and receive satisfaction: but you see, redemption cost him too. He denies himself and gives up the immediate management of all affairs into the hands of his

Son. The role of the Son was more intense though shorter, lasting not much more than thirty-three years. And though in a manner he remains hid till the day of judgment, even now Christ is all in all (Col. 3:12). The Son transacts all by the Spirit till the last day, and the Father works now only in and through the Son. Thus you see the Father veiling and eclipsing his glory, to make it shine the more hereafter, and in the meantime his love shines forth herein gloriously.

Does not the Father (as well as Christ) have a hand in sending the Holy Spirit to make a discovery and application of all these things? The Spirit is even called the *Promise of the Father*, which Christ had often hinted to his disciples as the best news he could bring them from heaven, (Acts 1:4).

Lastly, God wrapped all this up in a glorious covenant, a covenant of grace, life and peace, of which I may say as John of the commandment of love (1 John 2:7-8), that it is both the New and Old Covenant; the first and last and everlasting Covenant, a covenant of promise (Eph. 2:12). He has commanded this Covenant forever as in 2 Sam. 23:5, "he hath made with me an everlasting covenant, ordered in all things and secure," for this is all my salvation, and all my desire.

Chapter 6:
Presenting Yourself to God

Now all these things are phrased in the language of men, yet not without warrant from the Holy Ghost, who condescends to interpret the mysteries of salvation, else we could not understand it nor partake in it. And though they are all but one act in God, as all his attributes are but one divine excellency and glory, the divine essence itself, this is too big to come in all at once into our narrow hearts. Therefore God lets out himself by degrees as we may bear it. This is so not only in the discovery of himself, but also in the discovery of his counsel and operations concerning Christ Jesus.

Though many disown and dislike these things, I urge you to now go and put them home to God. And if he will own them and bear his witness to them, and seal them upon your heart, it will be sufficient to secure you from tormenting fears for time to come. I know he will work wonders rather than be lacking in his witness to so great a truth as this, and so shall you be delivered forever from your judge, from all frightful ideas and apprehensions of him as an angry severe judge and enabled to walk with him all your days, as with a most indulgent and tender-hearted Father. So now go, present your cause before him and fill your mouth with arguments; go, bow your knees to the God and Father of our Lord Jesus.

Tell him that he knows how your heart is pulled towards him according to the terms and tenor of a covenant of grace and not of works, a covenant which you cannot by any means secure.

He knows that the sole ground of your confidence is the precious and plenteous grace of the glorious Gospel of Jesus Christ, which demonstrates that Christ died for sinners, enemies, ungodly and impotent ones. Ask him if he ever had a soul with him in glory that was not once such a one as yourself? Many are ransomed and pardoned by Christ; so why cannot you be one of those many?

That salvation is neither of him that wills, nor of him that runs; but of God that shows mercy, (Rom. 9:16) even to the prisoners of unbelief, (Rom. 11:32).

Ask him if there is not a double reconciliation plainly taught in the doctrine of the Gospel? The one actually purchased by the death of Jesus Christ and acknowledged by God at that time; the other at the conversion of a sinner, when he lays down his arms and enmities, and the knowledge of the one is the means to the other.

Ask him why the Gospel should have been brought to your ears, your heart, without you trusting in it completely, even to the end (1 Peter 1:13). And if he called you to repentance, why would he now repent of his calling? For as Romans 11:29 states, his gifts and calling are, "without repentance."

Tell him he knows how fully, how thankfully your soul submits to that righteousness which is revealed in the Gospel. For none perish in unbelief except those who are either ignorant of the gospel message or do not submit to its calling (Rom. 10:3). Though you were once proud of your own righteousness, (that which Isaiah refers to in Isa. 64:6 as "filthy rags"), you have now cast that away with all your heart and soul for that most excellent provision made in the Gospel, and now appear continually before him clothed with that righteousness which Christ came on purpose to bring into the world, (Dan. 9:24).

He knows your heart closed with Christ for sanctification as well as righteousness to justify your faith and that there is nothing more desirable to your eye than that holiness which the Gospel requires, promises and promotes. He knows that you desire to reflect all his own glories, virtues, beauties and graces, so will he now break this glass in pieces?

Lastly, ask him if he will support that word spoken in his name by his servant Paul in Rom. 5:20, "where sin abounded, grace did much more abound." For God will make it good for the glory of his grace, wisdom and truth. Is not this the faith that should come? Or must you look for another? And if this be it, why then is not your heart purified, your heart and life sanctified by it? Why is it not unto you according to his word? (Acts 15:9, 26:18). Plead and press this hard upon him, and he will not deny you. You may take the Apostle Peter's word for it, that this is the true grace of God wherein you stand (1 Pet. 5:12).

Chapter 7: Overcoming Discouragement

But there is a damper upon your spirit, a great discouragement which reduces your boldness before him. You fear that though you believe and rejoice for a season in this grace, yet it is not likely to last always. You fear you will not be able to hold your joy and confidence to the end. But that when the snow melts away, you will find hypocrisy in your soul, and that there will be evil mixed with good. You fear that both the gift and grace, as well as the spirit of prayer will leave you as it did Job (Job 27:8-10). For what is the hope of the hypocrite, though he has gained, when God takes away his soul? Will God hear his cry when trouble comes upon him, will he delight himself in the Almighty? Will he always call upon God? Well, go to God in this case as well. Go order your cause before him and fill your mouth with arguments.

Tell him that he, and he alone knows whether or not you aim with your whole heart to keep yourself from iniquity, that you do not balk at any one of his commandments, and the more pure his word is, the more your soul loves it.

And also as to the means of grace, they are all dear and precious to you. Is this the guise of a hypocrite? Only be sure that your own heart does not deceive you.

He knows that is the purpose for living. And that you don't desire to be content to continue in this world without doing some good in your station and generation. Can this be the stance of a hypocrite?

He knows you would rather be sickly or poor or disgraced, as long as you can walk close with him than to have health, wealth, or honor but wander from him. He knows that you would rather follow hard after him even if you never enjoy his glorious, ravishing presence while here on earth than to swim in an abundance of carnal enjoyments, and to have a heart estranged from him. Is this the desire of any hypocrite in the world?

Tell God sincerely that you would rather he know all your secret sins against him, more than he should not know all your desires after him.

Tell him it would not be honorable of him to reject you, for all your secret prayers and pursuits after him must be known one day. And what would angels and men think to see such a mourner in secret cast off to all eternity?

Finally, appeal to him, for he knows you have been as earnest with him for holiness in times of prosperity as well as in times of straits and adversity: and is this the manner of hypocrites? Surely no. Jehoshaphat sought the Lord God of his Fathers, and walked in his commandments, and not after the backslidings of Israel. Therefore the Lord established the kingdom in his hand, and all Judah brought him presents, and he had riches and honor in abundance. And his heart was lifted up in the ways of the Lord.

Perhaps you may say, though I am no hypocrite, I am no better than a slave. I fear I am moved only by a spirit of fear, and this is far from a Gospel spirit, from a spirit of adoption. They are set as adversaries one against another: and if there were not a dread of God upon my spirit, if destruction from God were not a terror to me, I do not know what would become of me, nor whether Satan and my corruptions would overtake me. Then go and order your cause before him by prayer and fill your mouth with arguments.

Ask him if he has not observed your spirit to be more melted and humbled when he has filled your heart with joy and your mouth with praises than by any evil felt or feared. Is this the position of a slave or of a child?

Tell him it is true that you fear him, as do all the saints and angels in heaven, but such a fear enlarges your heart towards him; such a fear furthers the comforts of the Holy Ghost; such a fear has no torment in it. And therefore love though perfected shall never cast it out.

Tell him it is him and his goodness that you fear. His frown, his absence, his silence are now more dreaded by you than all his darts and thunders were formerly. The loss of his smile, his kiss, his kindness is what you most fear and this you take to be a spirit of your genuine relationship and not of slavery.

He knows your voice and can tell whether he hears any of his own language from you or not, however badly and broken it may be, (Isa. 38:14).

Every creature conveys its sound, its tone and tune to its young ones, and none of his children are stillborn. The Spirit unties their tongues and sets them crying Abba Father. He knows you cry to him, not as a thief before a judge whom he neither loves nor has any confidence in, but as a poor child when in distress who daily asks his Father's blessing.

Oh, but your backslidings and failures are many. How shall he pardon you for all this? God pauses, stands to consider how to include you among his children. "How will you plead with me, you that have transgressed against me?" says the Lord. When the Holy Spirit of God is grieved, where can you find another friend to speak a good word for you? When the Father is offended, the Son mediates for you. And when Christ is disobliged, the Spirit intercedes for you. But when the Spirit is vexed, there is no fourth person in the Trinity to make up the breach and to bridge the difference. Who then can put words into your mouth or fill your mouth with arguments? Still, even in this case you must try him, to see if he will not help you at this moment and prove to be an advocate for you. For he himself hath penned a prayer for one in your case, (Hosea 14:1-3). Go then even to this Holy Spirit and fill your mouth with arguments.

Tell him you have read or heard of his goodness, (Psa. 143:10), and of his love, (Rom. 15:30). Not only that which he begets in the saints, but that which he bears to them. All the world has had experience of it, the Church especially. And you are not altogether a stranger to it, having now occasion further to try it and to find it.

Ask him if it is possible for you to be in a worse situation than when he first found you? And will he now forsake the work of his own hands? (Psa. 138:8).

You hope he will stay with you when death has done its worst to you and then raise you again, according to Rom. 8:11. So will he now forsake your soul and not raise it again, now that sin and the devil have done their worst against it?

Have not the most eminent saints that he ever called had their periods of backslidings, sinning against that grace wherein lay their excellency? Were they all restored by him, and shall you only be abandoned? "I will heal their backslidings, I will love them freely, for mine anger is turned away from him," (Hosea 14:4).

He knows that nothing in the world ever so wounded you or went so near your heart as your tempting and grieving him has done. And you are resolved never to forgive yourself, even though he does and has.

Little did you think when God first turned your heart to himself, that there had been in it that which since broke forth from it, nor was any ever so deceived in you as you have been in yourself but are resolved now against that folly of trusting in your own heart any more.

Ask him upon what terms he first entered your heart. Was it not with a commission there to stay, however treated or entertained? Christ confirms it was agreed on in John 14:16, "And I will pray the Father, and he shall give you another Comforter, that he may abide with you forever."

The first Adam had him in his state of innocence, concurring merely as a third Person in the Trinity. But as for you, he must never leave you. He must not only alight but abide also, as upon the head, so upon the members, (John 1:32-33).

Say to the Spirit that you know he is God indeed, equal to the Father and the Son. And that though all the world should conspire against him, his invincible patience and good will must still raise an everlasting pillar of witness in your bosom. Let those who will cast him off do so but affirm that he shall be your God forever. "Who is a God like unto thee, pardoning iniquities," Micah 7:18. This scripture is equally true of the Father, the Son, and the Holy Spirit.

Ask him whether or not this one great end is why our nature was taken into personal union with the divine, that the diseases of the one might be healed by the infinite virtue, purity, and efficacy of the other? Did Christ come only to cure the sicknesses of the body or were not all these cures the types and representations of those he came to work upon the souls of sinners? Surely those who touch him by faith shall have their soul's diseases healed.

Did He not die that sin might die and be destroyed? Why does sin then live, seeing Christ died?

Demand even of justice, whether Christ has not fully paid your ransom? Why then are you kept in bonds? Why are you still bound by the cords of your sin? As Prov. 5:22 says, "his own iniquities shall take the wicked himself, and he shall be holden with the cords of his sins."

Complain that these corruptions defile and outrage that nature which Christ now wears in heaven and has exalted far above the brightest cherub. For he and his are all of one piece, (Heb. 2:11).

If there is any beginning of that everlasting work of sanctification in you, how then can he hide himself from his own flesh? He who established a law that a man should not hide himself when he saw his enemy's beast sink down under his burden, (Exod. 23:5). Does he care for oxen and donkeys and yet refuse to help the soul of one that loves him?

But perhaps you may think that through grace you may be both pardoned and purified in time, but it will cost you dearly first. A world of afflictions must be expected where there has been such a world of provocations, and yet remains such a mass of corruption. And these fears of what may come keep you from enjoying what is present. Go with this complaint to your judge that these fears may be disarmed, left powerless to distress you. Go fill your mouth with arguments, for who can say his mountain is strong, so he shall never be moved? Or who can foretell or foresee the things that may come upon him.

Tell him that whatever comes, it is your desire to bear his indignation, because you have sinned against him (Micah 7:9), because you know you have despised his judgments *all too often*. But tell him you would rather be under the disciplined schooling of his children than the boasting of his castaways. You would rather bear the severe mercy of his discipline than be ignored by him as those desperate lost souls whom God has given over to Satan. For his correcting rod as well as his supporting staff shall be a comfort to you (Psa. 23:4).

Though it be infinitely more desirable to be humbled and reformed than not at all, if he will be pleased to spare you, it would be more for his honor to do it in the midst of prosperity, because this is more difficult and more unusual

(Jer. 22:21). What glory it will be to him to discipline you in the midst of prosperity!

As this will be more glorious for him, so more useful to others. The examples of such a convert are much more conspicuous and illustrious, for in those who are troubled it is sometimes hard to distinguish between a devastation and a reformation, between their trouble for sin and for suffering, (Gal. 2:14).

Tell Him however he will go with you through fire and water, according to his gracious promise, (Isa. 43:2), that you are not afraid to venture, that you will interpret it to be his affection as well as his faithfulness, his magnifying of you, his setting his heart upon you, (Job 7:17-18). You will see it as his utmost kindness to you, seeing he himself styles it so. For blessed is the man whom you chasten, O Lord. Teach him out of your law, that you may give him rest from the days of adversity (Psa. 94:12-13). This then is a blessed condition, when correction and instruction are linked together and you cannot be happy without it, nor have you been over-eager after deliverance, when in affliction you have enjoyed his precious presence.

But it is hard to keep this mind when it comes to the trial, especially when God puts forth his hand and touches the quick, when he touches the bone and the flesh. As the devil said of Job, he will never endure that, "he will curse thee to thy face," (Job 2:5).

In extremity of pain when your spirit is ready to fail before him, and the soul which he has made is apt to say, "where is all that sweetness and tenderness you boasted of?

Where is now your fear, your confidence, the uprightness of your ways and your hope?" Yet even then labor to order your cause before him and fill your mouth with arguments. And if our hearts do not reproach us, if they do not condemn us for being secret atheists and notorious rebels, we may have boldness and freedom of speech in all these cases, (1 John 3:21). In this case it is a shameful thing for a professed Christian to know no other way of complaint or cure then a beast does, (Hosea 7:14), for a Christian indeed has a spiritual way of complaining, which affords more ease then the natural.

So therefore in case of pain, justify him and tell him you know that he exacts from you less than your iniquity deserves. Tell him those parts that feel the pain have deserved infinitely more than they feel; call to mind those times and places in which they have provoked the eyes of his glory, the wicked devices of your head, the wretched desires of your heart, the pollutions of your hands, the swiftness of your feet to do evil. Confess that the whole body deserves to be laid upon the rack in hell.

Be bold to remind him how utterly useless you are to him unless he fills and furnishes you with strength and patience to glorify him in suffering. Ask him if he can take any pleasure in your pain; whether that would be agreeable to the incomparable sweetness of his good nature? For would even the harshest parent beat a child all day and all night without intermission? In this way Hezekiah reasons from day even to night, *will you make an end of me?* I thought though sorrow may endure for a night, joy comes in the morning. But as Isa. 38:12-13 states, "as a lion, so will he break all my bones, from day even to night wilt thou make an end of me." Can this severity be consistent with the sweetest relations?

Ask him then with this complaint of Job's, "is it good to you that you should oppress, that you should despise the work of your hands? Thine hands have made me and fashioned me together round about, yet you destroy me. Remember I beseech you, that you have made me as the clay, and will you bring me to dust again?" (Job 10:3, 8-9). Or if that could be his pleasure and his pastime (which surely it is not), ask him if you are a fit match or mark for him? Am I a sea, or a whale, that you set a watch over me? (Job 7:12). Perhaps there is a Leviathan or Behemoth that may be a fit subject for him that made him, to make his sword proud to kill; but I am not so. Is my strength the strength of stones, or is my flesh of brass? Of course not. For I would soon crumble under his fingers if he hides his face from me or counts me among his enemies. So ask him, would you break a poor leaf driven by the wind? Or would you pursue dry stubble? Cease from troubling me, and let me alone, that I may take a little comfort.

And will he not be intreated? Remind him that he himself told you that he does not afflict willingly, nor grieve the children of men, to crush under his feet all the prisoners of the earth (Lam. 3:33-34). And if not the children of men, then certainly not the children of God, his own children.

If he will not crush the prisoners of earth, then certainly neither will he destroy the free-born citizens of heaven, those whom the Son made free. For he tells us we are free indeed if we are a prisoner of hope.

Ask him, why did he take pleasure in the pains of his dear Son, crushing and bruising him as in a wine press? Surely that work in itself was not pleasing work to him, but only as it made way for that which is his pleasure, the exercise of love and mercy. That was but a means to this end, and in itself a bitter one to God himself.

Now why did he put him to grief if he received no satisfaction by it? Were not his head, and heart, and hands, and feet, and sides tormented, that yours might be spared? Surely the sins of all believers were punished and paid for to the full, in and by their Surety, that of Christ's gruesome and ghastly death on the cross.

There is a far greater degree of love expressed in his afflicting of his Son because he knows whereof we are made. He remembers that we are but dust. And that this was the only gateway to our ease and deliverance, allowing us to share in his holiness and enjoy a far more exceeding and eternal weight of glory.

For having found Him whom my soul loves, I would long to hold him and not let him go. I would not let him go without a blessing. But even more, I would have the blessing and keep him too, his presence being the best of blessings. But woe to me when he departs from me.

Now though this is the most undesirable condition that can befall you, it is neither desperate nor unusual. So go therefore even in this case and order your cause before him and fill your mouth with arguments.

Tell him it is only fit that he should assert his own sovereignty, by coming or going when he pleases. But why should he take pleasure in being an absent God when he is your Savior, to be at his own house as a stranger who only stays for the night, seeing he alone is our hope and sole Savior in the time of trouble? "You O Lord are in the midst of us, and we are called by thy name, leave us not," (Jer. 14:8-9).

Be bold to remind him of those many engagements made by himself and his Son, never to leave you nor forsake you. Show him those promises like are found in John 14:21, "he that loveth me shall be loved of my Father, and I will love him and will manifest myself unto him," and verse 23, "my Father will love him, and we will come unto him, and make our abode with him," and, "Lord you know all things, you know that I love you," (John 21:17). Has he not said that He will not cast off his people, not even for all they have done against him? (Jer. 31:37). And if not for what they have done, what is there else that they need fear? "Fear not, you have done all this wickedness, yet do not turn aside from following the Lord." For the Lord will not forsake his people, seeing it pleased the Lord to make you his people; he can neither be less constant in his love, nor so mistaken in his choice, to be sorry for what he has done.

Tell the Sun of Righteousness it is true that you cannot bear his radiance nor his eclipses. But you would much rather choose to be burned up by his flames of embrace than to be frozen and starved in the shadow of his absence and the withdrawing of his favor.

Tell him that if you had never known him, you could have been without him, or at least without any present sense of sorrow for his absence. But now having tasted that he is gracious and in his favor is life, now knowing that his lovingkindness is better than life, you cannot bear to be one day without him.

Tell him he will certainly have a more sure return at the last than at the first, for all those who belong to him are never to hold their peace day or night, that all those who make mention of the Lord will not keep silent and will give him no rest, until he establishes and makes Jerusalem his dwelling place and place of worship and praise in the earth, (Isa. 62:6-7).

Inquire of him as to why Christ was forsaken by him, and yet Christians might never be so. Christ himself put the question to him from the cross, "My God, my God, why hast thou forsaken me?" Tell him you hope those living words of his dying Son made so deep an impression that they will never be out of his mind, never be forgotten.

Yet some may complain that though God is pleased to spare me both as to soul and body, his hand is against me in terms of my relations, friends, name, and estate, which are no insignificant matters. And in doing so he has served me a bitter cup. In this case go to him, order your case before him, and fill your mouth with arguments.

Does he threaten the removal of some near and dear relationship? Then tell him they are pieces of yourself. And is he now about to rend the very fabric of your heart?

He knows that the last corruption mortified in his children is our inordinate attachment to and affection for our close relationships. Is it so difficult then to die to those we love and release them to eternity?

Tell him he knows that you embraced such as tokens and favors of his love. These are the friends, the comforts which God has graciously given you, and that you now fear he is about to take them away in anger. Ask him if it pleases him to take them from you, will he be pleased to stand in the breach and to fill that void himself. He says he offers himself as such in Heb. 12:7, courting you to accept his company. And if he will make good on his offer, you know he shall be better to you than ten of those relations, friends, comforts, yea, than ten thousand of those whom he first lent you or put into your hand to hold for him and now has seen fit to call away from you.

He knows that though your connection to his creatures has cost you dearly, yet it has been the endeavor of your soul to live to him alone. And in the midst of all other comforts, your pursuit has been to make him your all, above all, with all, who shall hereafter be all, without all. And that in the meantime, you might live to him without the comforts of other relationships if it pleases him to strip you of them, knowing there was a worm at the root of those gourds, which would one day have deprived you of their refreshing shadow. He knows that sometimes when friends have failed, though at first you were shocked and hurt, yet upon reflection you rejoiced to find yourself laid at his door alone for help, and there have found him alone all-sufficient for you, doing for you then what he would not have done in consort with second causes. For you are well aware that it is foolish to take more of what is less while being content with less of what is most; a state which you will never be in while you live through his grace.

Yet you may say that though he spares the main branches, I am often afraid of losing what is dear to me by some particular unexpected providences. A little core of fear or trouble soon darkens the whole circumference of joy and pleasure, and then suddenly and many times the whole of heaven is black with clouds and wind, when at first nothing appeared but a little cloud. Why would you say as did Solomon in 1 Kings 5:4, "Now the Lord my God hath given me rest on every side, so that there is neither adversary nor evil occurrence," if you do not know how soon you may meet with many adversaries? Still, in this case go to your God, order your cause before him, and fill your mouth with arguments.

Ask him if your dependance is not on him alone for direction, for success in all your undertakings and concerns. He knows you have no other friend to rely on for counsel or assistance, "Thou wilt keep him in perfect peace, whose mind is stayed on thee, because he trusts in thee," (Isa. 26:3).

He is pleased to make our faith the rule of his favor, and as it were to give himself captive into the hands of our faith, to be such unto us as we would have him to be. As Christ said to the centurion in Matthew 8:13, "Go thy way and according as thou hast believed, so be it done unto thee."

Beg him to likewise say these words to you, for he knows what you have believed on through him.

Has it not been your manner to go to him and beg him to go with you even in your ordinary and smallest matters? We seek him in regard to those great matters, but we often think the small ones are within our own mastery, that we need not trouble him about those. But this is not so. And it is not so of you.

For you come to him with all your thoughts and plans, seeking that he would choose for you as if you are unfit and unable to choose for yourself. For you know he cannot choose amiss. So tell him you would cast yourself upon him, begging for mercy and direction in that very thing which hangs now like a thick cloud over your head and threatens you with storms and tempests. Then you may begin to rejoice in that providence, in that relation, in that business as dropped from your Father's hand.

Ask him if he must now be ashamed of your hopes and repent of your rejoicings and the good thoughts you have conceived of him? Shall you find a stone instead of bread, and instead of a fish, a serpent? No, one who knows him better than you do, has assured you of the contrary, (Luke 11:10-11), and therefore even the worst situation shall in time prove an advantageous affliction to you instead of a curse.

Chapter 8:
Dealing with God in Affliction

But some sad soul may ask, what will it help me even if no rod touches me outwardly, all the while in the mean time I lie under the lash of spiritual judgments, much blindness of mind, hardness of heart, deadness, coldness, distractions, insensibleness of spirit in holy duties, under heavenly ordinances, barrenness, unprofitableness, unsuitableness to all the cost and care and pains that God bestows on me. If this is your plight, then order your cause before him and fill your mouth with arguments.

Go tell him that of all judgments, he knows that spiritual ones are the most dreadful though least sensible, for though these are judgments from him they are sins in us, and sin is the worst of evils, even the only evil.

These judgments evidence that there is no union with Christ, no screen between the soul and wrath, as the earth which bears thorns and briars is rejected and nigh unto cursing, whose end is to be burned. They who are not for fruit must be for fuel; if not for bearing, for burning.

Plead therefore as for your life, that unless he means to damn you eternally, he would make all his ordinances helpful, sweet, successful, precious, and profitable to you.

Remind him that in the visible creation, all light is a kind of flame, though very thin and exceedingly subtle. This is undeniably true of the light of the sun, which being contracted and thickened in a glass can result in fire. Now why is it not so in the new creation? Are you not a child of the day? Is not the Sun of Righteousness risen upon you? Why then is there not heat proportionate to all the light that you enjoy? Why should the hardness of your heart be increased by it rather than abated?

Be bold to remind him that such is the energy and efficacy of his law of nature, that the characteristics of some fruits when they are in season are of a more lively red then at other times. And has he not also created powerful laws in regard to matters of his invisible creation as he did in the visible? Are there no spirits in his spiritual appointments? No law to make our spirits move and stir in those seasons of love and grace? Why do the wonders of nature remain, when those of grace seem to cease? We ourselves find our spirits move and stir with wonderful excitement and delight at our near approach to some dear relations; why should not our souls feel the same when we draw near to our best friends? Our dearest Father, sweetest Savior, only comforter? David felt it, as he mentions in Psa. 122:1-2, "I was glad when they said unto me, let us go into the house of the Lord, our feet shall stand within thy gates O Jerusalem."

Remind him that one of his crown jewels, his peculiar prerogative, is to teach his people so as to profit, (Isa. 38:17). And if he is the teacher, it does not matter who the scholar is. There is no one who teaches like him, (Job 36:22).

Remind him of his promise, not only that he will teach, but passively that his people shall be taught, (John 6.:45), especially the humble. God will not allow you to be proud on any terms, he will rather have you humbled by your sins than proud of your grace.

Remind him of his practice all along from creation to this day, which of all his saints none could say as well as David, "Thou O God has taught me from my youth up until now," (Psa. 71:17). Now put it to him and say, "Lord, will you not be my God to teach and to instruct me? To make me wise to salvation? For this also must come from him who is wonderful in counsels and excellent in working.

His goodness puts another argument in your mouth. As in Psa. 119:68, "Thou art good and do good. O teach me thy statutes."

He knows it is the devil and his agents which distract and disturb you, and would any parent allow his slave to abuse his child before his face, when he is upon his knee for a blessing, or comes to receive his commands? Ask him how he can allow his slave the devil to insult you before his face? Tell the Lord your God, the only true God, the living God, it will not be for his honor that you should continually be baffled and abused by Satan when you set yourself to worship him, with him looking on, who alone is able to rescue and relieve you, whose glory the devil strikes at, as well as at your peace and safety.

Tell him, if he will allow you nothing but the comfort of obedience to sweeten your nearness to him, that, that shall not dissuade you. His work on earth as well as in heaven is both work and wages. For in keeping his commandments there, "is great reward," (Psa. 19:11).

And when at any time you are afraid of being utterly disregarded, from a sermon, from a sacrament, from praying ground, say secretly in your heart, "Lord I am here; your poor servant whom you know so well, lo here I am. Is there not one word? Not one look? Not one touch this day in this duty?"

Say with Judges 1:15, "Give me a blessing, for you have led me through dry land, give me also springs of water. Give me the upper springs and the nether springs, and it will be well with me if I find you here."

Chapter 9: Will God Hear Me?

Some may say that all these pleadings may prove in vain, for I have thoughts and oppressing fears that a God so high, holy, and happy is not at all concerned with the distresses and distractions of man, no more than a man minds the movings or murmurings of flies or bees. So sometimes I find no answer at all, or one so strange and contrary that my fears are strengthened and confirmed.

Now though this temptation cannot prevail if you are a *constant* pleader with God, yet it is needful when it does show itself to go and order your cause before him and fill your mouth with arguments against it.

Remember how God himself affirms the contrary and tell him that you dare not question the truth of his engagements, "Though the Lord be high yet hath he regards the lowly, he does not at all forget himself when he remembers thee," (Psa. 138:6). No, he sets forth himself in all his glory when he professes the greatest kindness and condescension to those who judge themselves least capable of it, "Thus saith the high and lofty one that inhabits eternity, whose Name is Holy, I dwell in the high and holy place," (Isa. 57:15). Here's enough to make all the creatures that should hear it exceedingly fear (as is said of Moses, Heb. 12:21) and yet what follows? A soft still voice after all this thunder? "I dwell also with him that is of a broken and humble spirit, to revive the spirit of the humble and to revive the heart of the contrite ones," so that he who is brought below the condition of a creature broken and crumbled to nothing, may yet be a companion for this high and holy One. So Isa. 66:2, "though heaven be my throne and earth my footstool, yet to this man will I look that is poor and of a contrite spirit, and that trembles at my word." Tell him now, with a holy plainness and boldness, that he has ensnared himself with the words of his mouth, and he cannot go back. Besides, you have no reason to think he has any inclination to do so. "Lord thou hast heard the desire of the humble," (Psa. 10:17), and, "he will regard the prayer of the destitute and not despise their prayer," (Psa. 102:17).

Tell him that it is true that the distance is vast, and wide, and infinite between you and him, and yet he has given you opportunity to commune with him. Tell him that as a parent is often more taken with his little one's lisping and ill attempt at language than they would be with fluency of words, so infinitely more does the Lord show tenderness toward them that fear him. As Nehemiah pleads, "O Lord I beseech thee let now thine ear be attentive to the prayer of thy servant, and to the prayer of thy servants, who desire to fear thy name," (Neh. 1:11).

Tell him that your conscience, as well as your books (and the scriptures as well) assure you that he takes notice every time you sin against him, so why not every time you pray and seek after him? As in Psa. 139:5, "O Lord thou hast searched me and known me." Christ even as man with his human eyes sees all the wrongs we do or suffer, hears all our prayers with his ears, records all our doings; because Christ's glorified human nature, having personal union with the Son of God, may not be measured or bounded by other men's faculties or imperfection. "The Man Christ Jesus is Mediator," (1 Tim. 2:5), and, shall be *Judge*, (Acts 17:31). And if the man Christ Jesus hears you, will he not answer graciously?

Tell him that most men are quick of hearing, when anything is said that pleases them and ask him whether he is more ready to attend to what's most contrary than what's most agreeable to him? That which gives occasion to execute vengeance, (Isa. 28:21), or to exercise mercy, delight, and pleasure, (Micah 7:18). He professes to listen and hearken after the language of repentance, (Jer. 8:6), after holy conference, (Mal. 3:16). As 1 John 5:14-15, "And this is the confidence that we have in him, that if we ask any thing according to his will he heareth us, and if we know that he hears us, whatsoever we ask, we know that we have the petitions that we desired of him." And Isaiah 59:1-2, "Behold the Lord's hand is not shortened that it cannot save, neither his ear heavy that it cannot hear; but your iniquities have separated between you and your God, and your sins have hidden his face from you, that he will not hear."

Tell him you must not only go contrary to your conscience but also to your experience to suspect him, for you cannot but acknowledge that many a time he has been near you in all the things you have called on him for, (Deut. 4:7). And this nearness to God in prayer when you come to thank him for mercies has not only renewed that sweetness, it has exceeded it. This experience you have had of nearness to God in prayer, you know that God has heard you, he has attended to the voice of your prayer. Therefore, you may say, "in the day when I cried you answered me, and strengthened me with strength in my soul," (Psa. 138:3).

And that's the best experience of answer to prayer. Therefore you cannot call his hearing in question, unless you would complain as in John 9:16, "If I had called and he had answered, yet would I not believe that he had answered my voice," looks like the language of a most obstinate and invincible unbelief, as when a man will not believe his petition has been granted, though he see it granted. Yet I will never believe that it is for any worthiness in me or them, no it is not to my voice, but to the voice of a good Friend of mine, my Mediator that God hearkens, and for his sake he so graciously answers. "Wait therefore patiently for the Lord, and he will incline unto thee and hear thy cry," (Psa. 40:1). He never yet prepared any heart to pray that he did not also ready his ear to hear (Psa. 10:17).

Ask the Lord Jesus if it is not his work to reconcile? Indeed when the great day of his wrath is come it will be so, and who then shall be able to abide it? But remind him, that the wisdom which is from above is gentle and easy to be intreated (James 3:17), and shall you not find the essential wisdom of the Father to be so? The heart of Christ is as fit a receptacle for our sorrows of all sorts as the eye is of colors, and is it shut up in endless displeasure against you only? As Zeph. 3:17 says, "The Lord thy God in the midst of thee is mighty: he will save, he will rejoice over thee with joy: he will rest in his love, he will joy over thee with singing." What more can be said to assure you of his delighting in you?

Does not the sweet savor of Christ's sacrifice, the odor of his intercession, so diffuse itself and fill heaven that the stench of your sins cannot enter? Surely were it not for that perfume, God could never endure the stinking dunghill of this world so near him, as smoke in his nostrils all day.

Plead the words of Christ himself, as in Matt. 18:13, that the owner of the flock looks with more joy, pleasure, and delight upon a poor stray sheep that is recovered than upon the whole flock that never ran that hazard. And has not Christ had you in his arms and in his bosom and upon his shoulder for a long time, to bring you back to his fold and favor? It is a recovering church and people which Christ is so taken with, one that had been forsaken and desolate whom the Lord is said to delight in, as in Isa. 62:4, "Thou shalt no more be termed forsaken and desolate, but thou shalt be called Hephzibah, for the Lord delights in thee."

To be certain, he takes no pleasure in the death of him that dies more than he takes pleasure in the life of him who through his abundant rich grace in Christ Jesus recovers. As Ezek. 33:10-11 states, "Therefore O thou Son of Man, speak unto the house of Israel. Thus ye spoke, saying, 'If our transgressions and our sins be upon us, and we pine away in them, how should we then live?' Say unto them, 'As I live,' saith the Lord God, 'I have no pleasure in the death of the wicked, but that the wicked turn from his way and live. Turn ye, turn ye from your evil ways, for why will ye die O house of Israel.'"

Ask whether he sees you in your present state and station or as you shall be through all eternity? For to him who sits in that high tower of eternity, nothing is past or future but all things are alike in one perpetual now, present before him. Now within a little while Christ will present to himself, and then to his Father, a glorious Church not having spot nor wrinkle, nor any such thing, but holy and without blemish (Eph. 5:27). And if now he now sees you in that eternal mirror, he may well say, "you are all fair my love, there is no spot in you."

A supper, a feast is for delight and cheerfulness, and even until supper time Christ waits to be gracious, until the shadows of the evening be stretched out, as in Rev. 3:20, "Behold, I stand at the door and knock: if any man hear my voice, and open the door, I will come in to him, and will sup with him, and he with me." Does not your soul cry out to him, "Come in, blessed of the Lord, why do you stand without? Break open the door, if need be, so you, the King of Glory, might come in and dine with me."

Tell him that because of his infinite mercy now and again you feel his quickening, his ravishing presence and comfort while in the world. He knows the posture of your soul to be in small measure similar to that of David's in 2 Sam. 15:26, "But if he says, I have no delight in thee; behold, here am I, let him do to me as seems good to him."

If heaven above were brass, surely the earth below would be iron, and if there were no drawing in his heart toward you, surely there would be none in your heart towards him. You could never delight yourself in the Almighty if he took no delight in you, (Heb. 10:38-39).

And yet a generous and noble minded Christian may be ready to say that all this cannot, ought not, fully satisfy me though the Lord permit me to have such sweet secret communion with him, (for which I can never be sufficiently thankful). Yet if he will not honor me so as to use me and make me in some way serviceable in my generation, this is lamentable. This is that I fear – that I shall prove to be nothing more than a dry tree, an empty vine, that I will bring forth no fruit, do no good, neither find God working with me, nor be permitted to work with God. For every good warrior, every good magistrate, this is his greatest comfort, glory, and safety, that he works with God and God with him.

So Paul speaks of himself and his fellow-laborers in the ministry, that we are as workers together with him, (2 Cor. 6:1). This privilege reaches not only ministers but all professors and all those who are now the royal priesthood, (1 Peter 2:5, 9, Rev. 1:5), and even among good people. What man is able to bear being laid aside and cast off? How should you be able to bear such a trial, either to fall from your standing or to be unable to do any good though continued in it? If this is ever your case, go order your cause before him and fill your mouth with arguments.

Tell him you perceive it is not his will to destroy you, for if the Lord were pleased to kill you he would not have accepted an offering at your hand, neither would he have shown you all these things which he locks up from so many thousands, and yet has shared them with you. For you can say to him as with the prophet in Hab. 1:12, "Are you not from everlasting O Lord my God, my holy one, I shall not die." You are the King eternal. You do not change; therefore I am not, I shall not be consumed.

Plead upon this ground and tell him that it is not honorable to him to only keep you alive and make no use of you, to preserve your soul only as salt to preserve the body but allow you to do no service. Remind him that through his grace some sad sinners have proved to be most shining saints, as in Scripture the children of women long barren have proved most eminent instruments like Sarah who bore Isaac, Rachel who bore Joseph, Hannah who bore Samuel, Manoah's wife who bore Sampson, and Elizabeth who bore John the Baptist. So, if ever a soul desired to redeem the time and salvage what has been lost, then you much more; and it will be to the praise of the glory of his grace if he will help you do so.

He knows that you are now in the process of sanctification, and therefore it will be no dishonor to him to use and employ you. In fact, he has even published by the pen of his apostle, that if a man purge himself from that which defiles him, he shall be a vessel unto honor, sanctified and made meet for the master's use, *prepared unto every good work*, (2 Tim. 2:21).

Ask him if he did not call you and lead you to your present station, and will he now leave you to wither like a bulrush in the mire and to vanish away in utter unserviceableness? Who can take unto himself the honor of magistracy or ministry, or any other way of usefulness, but he who is called of God as was Aaron (Heb. 5:4). "Wherefore the Lord God of Israel saith, I said indeed that thy house, and the house of thy fathers should walk before me: but now the Lord saith, be it far from me; for them that honor me I will honor, and they that despise me shall be lightly esteemed," (1 Sam. 2:30).

Remind him how often you beg him never to trust you with advantages and opportunities unless he also gives you a heart to be faithful and fruitful in the fulfillment of them. Have you not prayed even against power and riches lest you should feel sufficient with these alone and deny him and say, who is the Lord? Have you not been in this regard sometimes more afraid of riches, honor, greatness, than their counterparts, lest you should not live unto him and to his service?

Remind him of that passage in Rom. 5:20, "Where sin abounded grace did much more abound," and how that makes you not only *not fear extraordinary judgments*, but even to *look for* extraordinary favors; having more love toward him, more humility, more holiness, more watchfulness; and by these, more than ordinary usefulness and serviceableness in your generation. As it is not his disposition to rebuke, (James 1:5), expect that he should give liberally of that wisdom to you, which may make you more serviceable in your station.

For it is a legitimate fear that God at last should turn his back on you, and you would then be found among those that are deceivers of their own souls, being turned into hell, when it seems their looks were toward heaven. If this is ever your situation, go to God presently, go fill your mouth with arguments.

Complain against your own heart, so far as there is any mixture of unbelief in this fear; and pray that his anger may not grow hot against you for asking him for so many signs, considering how often he has answered you previously, and especially considering that everything is at stake here. Eternity is before you, and if you are mistaken in your confidence, you are lost irrecoverably to all eternity. This consideration may move him to pity rather than to anger; and to say to them that are of a fearful heart, "be strong, fear not, behold your God will come and save you," (Isaiah 35:4).

Further, ask him if he has not made all as sure as grace can make it; indeed, it is all of grace, that the promise might be sure to all the seed, (Rom. 4:16), as sure as infinite love, infinite wisdom, infinite power, can make it, as you realize that the abomination of unbelief puts more affronts and scorn upon him than all other sins whatsoever.

Ask if all the spirits of just men now made perfect will not confess the mercies of Christ to be sure mercies, and that he (as Boaz said of Ruth) showed them more kindness in the latter end than at the beginning; and that having loved his own which were in the world he loved them to the end. David makes it obvious to any man's observation in Psa. 37:37, "Mark the perfect man, and behold the upright: for the end of that man is peace."

If you still fear, ask if the Holy Spirit (who makes it his trade to help infirmities and has certainly helped you throughout your whole life), ask if he will not then help you when you are nothing but a lump of infirmity and weakness. Surely then, in your greatest need he will not fail you.

Lastly, tell him he knows why you desire to be with him in his heaven, not because you fancy a place of paradise wrought with pleasures, and not just because you want to escape a place of everlasting burnings. Rather your soul longs incessantly for heaven because this is the land of hallelujahs for he abides there. And being in his presence would cause you to be most thankful.

Chapter 10: Looking Forward

Heaven is the place of pure and perfect love, where one is loved and loving without intermission, without interruption, eternally and ever with Christ. And this is far better (Phil. 1:23). Here you are met daily with a thousand hindrances and incumbrances which only make you long more for heaven as in 2 Cor. 5:2, "For in this we groan earnestly, desiring to be clothed upon with our house which is from heaven."

Hinderances and incumbrances, which make a hell above ground. How much more intolerable is the nethermost hell, for there is never a corner in it where a poor sinner might weep without blaspheming, without hearing blasphemies, without hating God, and without sinning against him. Your soul cannot bear the thought of losing him and all love to him, and to be sinning against him eternally. Nothing therefore short of heaven can satisfy you or ought to so do.

This hope then we have as an anchor of the soul both sure and steadfast, even Jesus our High Priest forever (Heb. 6:19-20). Therefore, build up yourselves on your most holy faith, and pray in the Spirit, keep yourselves in the love of God, and look for the mercy of our Lord Jesus Christ unto eternal life (Jude 20, 21).

Before parting, consider whether you can and should speak a good word for others also. This is the way of the spirit of adoption, as when David came before the Lord upon the saddest occasion that ever his soul was acquainted with, and yet he remembers Jerusalem in the midst of his greatest grief and prefers her before his chiefest joy. What his sins had weakened and attempted to ruin, he endeavors to strengthen and repair by his prayers. Seldom do you see him rise from his knees before he pleads the cause of God's people, and oftentimes he makes that his only errand, as you may find in several of his psalms.

Sometimes the best intercessors do not feel their own hearts warm in the work until they come out of the narrow circle of their own personal concerns and launch into the business of the body of Christ. Only then are their hearts fixed by the spirit of grace and supplication, the great soul of that body.

Plead for his poor persecuted people all over the world. Ask if it is nothing to him to see the blood of the martyrs of Jesus Christ, spilt like water upon the ground even to this day, in certain places around the globe? Are not the eyes of his glory weary of such sad spectacles? Ask if the rage with which these saints have been slain do not reach up to heaven (2 Chron. 28:9).

Complain that there's nothing visible towards a reckoning with that drunken beast, which makes itself drunk with the blood of the saints as with sweet wine. Inquire as to when the powers of the earth will melt like wax before the fire at the presence of the Lord? Why is his chariot so long coming? Remind him that the harvest of the earth is not only ripe, but even dried up and withered, (Rev. 14:15, Matt. 13:6). His patience is longsuffering, but how long Lord, holy and true? We hear as yet no noise, no shaking at all in the valley of dry bones, no coming together of the bones. Beg that he water his plantations abroad. You that have escaped the miseries that have befallen others, remember the Lord and his people afar off, and let Jerusalem come into your mind, (Jer. 51:50).

Complain to Him of that spirit of profanity which yet dominates our lands. He has given some into our hands, others under our feet. O pray that Christ may bless many nations, and ours among the rest, in a special manner with his blood and spirit, that we may yet become a peculiar people zealous of good works.

Press into him to cast out that unthankful spirit wherewith so many are possessed. We are ready to reel and dash one against another continually, many abusing, many despising all their present mercies. Jealousies and selfish pursuits keep many from praying for their leaders. And how can they look for good by them who sin in ceasing to pray for them? (1 Tim. 2:1-2). For our practice should be that of making supplications, prayers, intercessions, and giving of thanks for all men, for our rulers and for all that are in authority.

When shall the day dawn when the deaf hear the words of the book, and the eyes of the blind see out of obscurity and out of darkness? When will the Lord again make bare his holy arm? When will he smell, in our church assemblies, a savor of rest, and take pleasure in our solemn meetings, as in the days of old?

Deal earnestly with him about the compounding and compromising of our differences, distances, and divisions, which have given such a wound to religion, opened such a gap to Satan, which everyone complains of and yet helps to widen. Urge that all the children of light may walk more in the light, and he is in the light, and then shall we have fellowship one with another, (I John 1:7).

Few men currently honor the Lord with their substances, few look at this as a duty to consecrate any part of their gain or substance to the Lord, but rather behave as if they did not depend upon God and therefore no acknowledgment was due him. Surely God from the beginning reserved and claimed a part due to himself, who gave the whole, and whatever there was besides as Exod. 22:29 states, "Thou shalt not delay offering the first of thy ripe fruits and of thy liquors: the first born of thy sons shalt thou give unto me."

And all the tithe of the land, whether of the seed of the land, or of the fruit of the tree, it is the Lord's. It is holy unto the Lord, as it is his already, and has been so from the beginning of the world. To show honor and deference to the Creator, Giver, and Sustainer of all, the initial portion of every man's increase, acquisitions, improvements, and income is due unto the Lord and ought to be dedicated to God and to the everlasting priesthood of our Lord Jesus Christ. To this end, and to show thankful acknowledgement to God for the same, everyone (including even the ministers) ought to pay a tenth which should then be spent in the supporting of public worship, relieving of the poor at home and abroad, and for other worthy causes.

Do not withhold good from those to whom it is due, when it is in the power of your hand to do it. Don't say to your neighbor, "Come back tomorrow and I will give you what you need," when you have it with you now. What we call giving, God calls paying; what we call charity, he counts due debt. The decision we need to make is what portion of everything is due to God, and that portion that has long been held as his due standard is the tenth part (Heb. 7:4). Why else did Abraham pay tithes to Melchizedek (Gen. 14:20), one of the great representations of Christ in the Old Testament? (Heb. 7:2-3).

And as Heb. 7:5 states, these tithes were paid to the priesthood of Christ, and Levi and his sons, "who receive the office of the priesthood," for they were the receivers of said tithe. Abraham is a prime example, four hundred and thirty years before the Law (as the apostle observes on another occasion in Gal. 3:17). We also have the story of Jacob who vowed to give a tenth of all that God gave him, (Gen. 28:22). Further, Christ approves it, (Matt. 23:23), and affirms that dedicating a part to charitable uses sanctifies the whole, as the first fruit sanctified the lump, (Luke 11:41-42, 12:33). Christ teaches that we are to give unto God the things that are God's, (Mark 12:17), while remembering that both we and all that we have are his, (I Cor. 29:14), though he is pleased to accept a small part in lien of the whole.

I think there must also be some rule of proportion for that laying by in store commanded by the apostle, 1 Cor. 16:2, "Upon the first day of the week, let every one of you lay by him in store, as God hath prospered him, that there be no gatherings when I come," (according to Deut. 16:10). Now if there be no guidelines in terms of amount, a large heart may lay by too much and defraud his relations or other occasions, and a narrow heart would be sure to lay by too little, and so be guilty of sacrilege by alienating that which is due to God, to whom we owe an honorary tribute. Not that he needs it from us, but he requires it of us. And little comfort shall they have who deny returning to him what he requires of us.

This may seem too much elaboration on this point. But if the Lord would instill the sense of this duty upon the hearts and consciences of his children, how soon would there be a sacred bank, a stock raised, a treasury-filled temple to give a speedy relief to the necessities of saints abroad as well as at home.

How would this practice support the Gospel charge for fruitfulness in good works? "Let those who have believed in God be careful to maintain good works," (Titus 3:8). How would this practice bring a blessing and prove to be a hedge about all the rest of the estate, like Hannah's loaf which was lent to God, (1 Sam. 2.:20-21). He gave her back five for one, and so will he do by every one that ventures with him to prove him, (Mal. 3:10). But it is a snare for a man to devour that which is sanctified, (Prov. 20:25). Listen to God's words in Hosea 2:8-9, "For she did not know that I gave her corn, and wine, and oil, and multiplied her silver and gold which they prepared for Baal, they wasted all upon their lusts. Therefore will I return and take away my corn in the time thereof; and my wine in the season thereof, and will recover my wool, and my flax, given to cover her nakedness."

And who would regret his obedience here when he comes to die and to be torn away from all his outward enjoyments? It is then that men's consciences convict them. It is then that their hearts melt away with anguish and astonishment to think how they have served the devil with their estates and not God, to whom they are now going to give an account of their stewardship which he will entrust to them no longer.

But how we have embraced a cheap Christianity and we therefore like it because it saves our purses, though not our souls. What praying heart does not feel cause to go to God about it, and to fill his mouth with arguments?

Here I have only offered *hints to help* on this blessed work of pleading and striving and wrestling with God (with the arms of his own Spirit) in prayer. But still, how few stir up themselves to take hold of God (Isa. 64:7). Now it must needs be granted that the spirit of adoption is the best logician, the only One, both for invention and judgment, as it was he that taught Aristotle and others to reason with men, as well as Job and Jeremiah and the rest of the saints to reason out their case with God.

When the Spirit has formed the propositions according to the principles of truth laid down in Scripture and according to his office, he bears witness (1 John 5:6) by making application of the proposition to the person, and then clearly and strongly infers the conclusion.

All his arguments are highly satisfactory and grounded, such that he convinces of righteousness as well as of sin and subdues the soul to the obedience of faith. If we admit that the offices and duties of reconciliation and mediation and intercession belong to Christ, so the office of intercession also belongs to the Spirit and not exclusively to Christ, "The spirit itself makes intercession for us," (Rom. 8:26).

And dare I be bold to say that he who has none of that Spirit within him, who can find no help by the conscientious and constant use of his pleading, then I would advise that you select something out of every sermon you hear to be repeated upon your knees in secret, which posture I believe best both for repeating and studying anything of this nature.

And let me add that if God does not hear and answer you upon these terms, if this does not build strength to your faith to overcome, then you may even say that all the ministers of his holy gospel are sadly mistaken as Heb. 10:35 states, "Cast not away therefore this confidence [this privilege of speaking freely and pleading with your God], which has great recompence of reward."

Do not forget how he calls his people to come and reason out the matter with him and what he promises shall ensue, "Come now and let us reason together, saith the Lord: though your sins be as scarlet, they shall be as white as snow, though they be red like crimson, they shall be as wool," (Isa. 1:18). And for those who do not come under the guidelines or qualifications of this communication here mentioned, who cannot own any of these arguments, the Lord have mercy on them, for they cannot plead and will most assuredly be pressed to death for lack of it.

In this way have I brought you to peep through the keyhole, through the hole of the door into the tower of David. If you have felt the hand of Christ by the hole of the door, touching your heart, and if you have been moved for him, will you not be more so in this? You will not be at rest until you can be found arguing out the matter with him in secret daily.

And let me say assuredly that this exercise will infinitely surpass in sweetness all sports and pastimes, all the treasures and glories of this world, all the delights of the sons of men, for it is the delight of the Sons of God. This is heaven on earth, heaven on this side of heaven, and will undoubtedly convey you at last into that heaven of heavens where you will be overcome with joy and glory for evermore.

FINIS.

Published Works by Westminster Divines at Puritan Publications

1647 Westminster Confession of Faith 3rd Edition – KJV Bible

A Biblical Response to Superstition, Will-Worship and the Christmas Holiday by Daniel Cawdrey (1588-1664)

A Devotional on Our Savior's Death and Passion by Charles Herle (1598-1659)

A Discourse on Church Discipline and Reformation by Daniel Cawdrey (1588-1664)

A Glimpse of God's Glory by Thomas Hodges (1600-1672)

A Golden Topaz, or Heart-Jewel, Namely, a Conscience Purified and Pacified by the Blood and Spirit of Christ by Francis Whiddon (d. 1656)

A Sermon Against Lukewarmness in Religion by Henry Wilkinson (1566-1647)

A Treatise of the Loves of Christ to His Spouse by Samuel Bolton, D.D. (1606-1654)

A Treatise on Divine Contentment by Simeon Ashe (d. 1662)

A Vindication of the Keys of the Kingdom of Heaven into the Hands of the Right Owners by Daniel Cawdrey (1588-1664)

Armilla Catechetica, or a Chain of Theological Principles by John Arrowsmith (1602-1659)

Attending the Lord's Table by Henry Tozer (1602-1650)

Christ Inviting Sinners to Come to Him for Rest by Jeremiah Burroughs (1599-1646)

Christ the Settlement in Unsettled Times by Jeremiah Whitaker (1599–1654)

Family Reformation Promoted, and Other Works by Daniel Cawdrey (1588-1664)

God is Our Refuge and Our Strength by George Gipps (n.d.)

God Paying Every Man His Due by Francis Woodcock (1614-1649)

God With Us, and Other Works by John Strickland (1601-1670)

God, the Best Acquaintance of Christians by Matthew Newcomen (1610–1669)

God's Voice from His Throne of Glory by John Carter (d. 1655)

Gospel Peace, Or Four Useful Discourses by Jeremiah Burroughs (1599-1646)

Gospel Worship, or, The Right Manner of Sanctifying the name of God in General, in Hearing the Word, Receiving the Lord's Supper, and Prayer by Jeremiah Burroughs (1599-1646)

Gradual Reformation Intolerable by C. Matthew McMahon and Anthony Burgess (1600-1663)

Halting Stigmatized by Arthur Sallaway (b. 1606)

How to Serve God in Private and Public Worship by John Jackson (1600-1648)

Independency A Great Schism by Daniel Cawdrey (1588-1664)

Jacob's Seed and David's Delight by Jeremiah Burroughs (1599-1646)

Jesus Christ God's Shepherd by William Strong (d. 1654)

Making Religion One's Business by Herbert Palmer (1601-1647)

Presumptive Regeneration, or, the Baptismal Regeneration of Elect Infants by Cornelius Burgess (1589-1665)

Primitive Baptism and Therein Infant's and Parent's Rights by Matthew Sylvester (1636–1708)

Real Thankfulness by Simeon Ashe (d. 1662)

Reasonable Christianity by Henry Hammond (1605-1660)

Reformation and Desolation by Stephen Marshall (1594–1655)

Repentance and Fasting by Peter Du Moulin (1601-1684) and Henry Wilkinson (1566-1647)

Rules for Our Walking With God by Jeremiah Burroughs (1599-1646)

Salvation in a Mystery by John Bond (1612-1676)

Scripture's Self Evidence by Thomas Ford (1598–1674)

Selected Works of Peter Sterry by Peter Sterry (1613–1672)

Sermons, Prayers, and Pulpit Addresses Alexander Henderson (1583-1646)

Singing of Psalms the Duty of Christians by Thomas Ford (1598–1674)

Spots of the Godly and of the Wicked by Jeremiah Burroughs (1599-1646)

The All-Seeing Unseen Eye of God and Other Sermons by Matthew Newcomen (1610–1669)

The Art of Divine Meditation by Edmund Calamy (1600-1666)

The Art of Happiness by Francis Rous (1579–1659)

The Certainty of Heavenly and the Uncertainty of Earthly Treasures by William Strong (d. 1654)

The Christian's Duty Towards Reformation by Thomas Ford (1598–1674)

The Church's Need of Jesus Christ by Thomas Valentine (1586-1665)

The Covenant of Life Opened by Samuel Rutherford (1600-1661)

The Covenant of Works and the Covenant of Grace by Edmund Calamy (1600-1666)

The Covenant-Avenging Sword Brandished by John Arrowsmith (1602-1659)

The Difficulties of and Encouragements to a Reformation by Anthony Burgess (1600-1663) 2nd Ed.

The Doctrine of Man's Future Eternity by John Jackson (1600-1648)

The Efficiency of God's Grace in Bringing Gain-Saying Sinners to Christ by Simeon Ashe (d. 1662)

The Eternity and Certainty of Hell's Torments by William Strong (d. 1654)
The Excellency of Holy Courage in Evil Times by Jeremiah Burroughs (1599-1646)

The Excellent Name of God by Jeremiah Burroughs (1599-1646)

The Fall of Adam and Other Works by John Greene (d. 1660)

The Glorious Name of God the Lord of Hosts by Jeremiah Burroughs (1599-1646)

The Worthy Churchman, or the Faithful Minister of Jesus Christ by John Jackson (1600-1648)

The Zealous Christian by Simeon Ashe (d. 1662)

Zeal for God's House Quickened by Oliver Bowles B.D. (1574-1664?)

Zion's Joy by Jeremiah Burroughs (1599-1646)

The Glory and Beauty of God's Portion and Other Sermons by Gaspar Hickes, (d. 1677)

The Godly Man's Ark by Edmund Calamy (1600-1666)

The Growth and Spreading of Heresy by Thomas Hodges (1600-1672)

The Guard of the Tree of Life, a Discourse on the Sacraments by Samuel Bolton (1606-1654)

The Light of Faith and Way of Holiness by Richard Byfield (1598–1664)

The Manifold Wisdom of God Seen in Covenant Theology by George Walker (1581-1651)

The Nature, Danger and Cure of Temptation by Richard Capel (1586–1656)

The Necessity, Dignity and Duty of Gospel Ministers by Thomas Hodges (1600-1672)

The Precious Seeds of Reformation by Humphrey Hardwicke (n.d.)
The Puritans on Exclusive Psalmody Edited by C. Matthew McMahon

The Rock of Israel and Other Sermons by Edmund Staunton (1600-1671)

The Saint's Communion With God by William Strong, A.M. (d. 1654)

The Saint's Inheritance and the Worldling's Portion by Jeremiah Burroughs (1599-1646)

The Saint's Will Judge the World, and Other Sermons by Daniel Cawdrey (1588-1664)

The Sermons of William Spurstowe (1605-1666)

The Soul's Porter, or a Treatise on the Fear of God by William Price (1597-1646)

The Spiritual Chemyst, or Divine Meditations on Several Subjects by William Spurstowe (1605-1666)

The Sweetness of Divine Meditation by William Bridge (1600-1670)

The Trial of a Christian's Sincere Love to Christ by William Pinke (1599–1629)

The Wells of Salvation Opened by William Spurstowe (1605-1666)

www.ingramcontent.com/pod-product-compliance
Lightning Source LLC
Chambersburg PA
CBHW031002090426
42737CB00008B/646